CW00767333

The Westmorland Dales Walking Handbook

60 Walks in Kirkby Stephen district, Stainmore, Orton Fells, Smardale, Ravenstonedale, northern Howgills and the Upper Eden Upland of Hartley Fell, Mallerstang, Wild Boar Fell and The Clouds

Peter McWilliam

westmorland-dales.co.uk

Published by Peter McWilliam, Kirkby Stephen,
Cumbria

©Peter McWilliam

All maps and photographs by the author

First published 2018

ISBN 978-0-9955263-4-1

Printed by Ashford Colour Press, Gosport,
Hampshire

The Westmorland Dales Walking Handbook

Contents

Section 1
Kirkby Stephen & Stainmore
1. Greenriggs & Croglam
2. Two Eden footbridges
3. Waitby & Greenriggs
4. Hartley & Winton
5. Stenkrith Park
6. Sandwath
7. Jubilee Nature Park & Nateby
8. Smardale, Soulby & Winton
9. Settle-Carlisle Station (KSW)
10. Kirkby Stephen Town Trail
11. The Eden Viaducts Walk
12. Waitby & Smardale Mill
13. Lockthwaite & Nateby
14. South Stainmore
15. Kirkby Stephen to Pendragon
16. Kirby Stephen Poetry Path
Section 2
Orton Fells & Smardale
Location Map Walks 17 - 26
17. Smardale Gill & Fell
18. Great Asby Scar
19. Potts Valley & Lt. Asby Scar
20. Nettle Hill & Ladle Lane
21. Crosby Ravensworth Fell
22. Orton Scar & Knott
23. Ash Fell Edge
24. Great Ewe Fell
25. Oddendale & Hardendale
26. Great & Little Kinmond
Section 3
Ravenstonedale & N. Howgills
Location Map Walks 27 - 42
27. Green Bell
28. Smardale Br. & Newbiggin
29. Crosby Garrett Circular
30. Ash Fell
31. Smardalegill Viaduct
32. Paradise
33. Harter Fell & Wandale
34. Uldale Waterfalls
35. Randygill Top & Kensgriff
36. Cautley Spout & The Calf

Section 3 continued
37. Blease Fell
38. Uldale Head & Fell Head
39. Baugh Fell
40. Black Force, The Spout & Linghaw
Section 4
Upper Eden Upland; The High Fells of Hartley, Mallerstang, Wild Boar Fell and The Clouds
Location Map Walks 41 - 60
41. Ewbank Scar & Ladthwaite
42. Great Bell, Mallerstang
43. Wharton Common
44. The Clouds, Ravenstonedale
45. Hartley Birkett, Hartley Fell
46. Lord's Stone & Greyrigg
47. Tailbridge Hill
48. Wensleydale Borderland
49. The Dukerdale Circuit
50. The Nine Standards
51. Fells End Quarry & High Pike
52. Great Bell, Bleakham & High Pike
53. Elmgill Crag & Raven's Nest
54. Swarth & Wild Boar Fells from Garsdale
55. Wild Boar Fell from Wharton Fell
56. Mallerstang & Nine Standards Horseshoe
57. Mallerstang Edge
58. Sand Tarn & Wild Boar Fell
59. The Clouds, Ravenstonedale
60. The Nine Standards

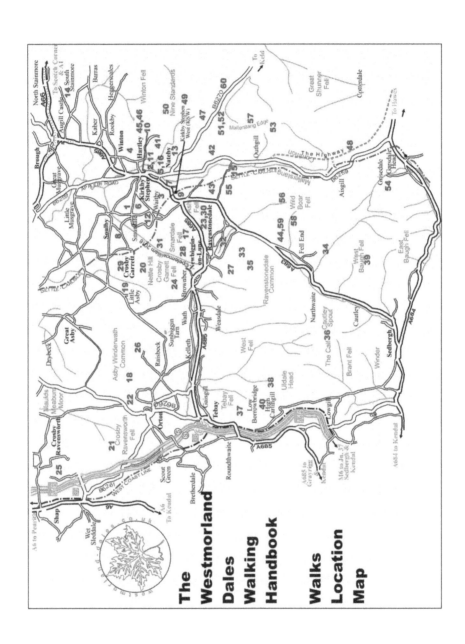

The
Westmorland
Dales
Walking
Handbook

Walks
Location
Map

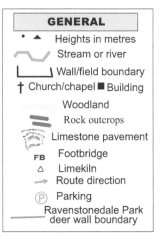

All the walks in this book have been published previously by the author and remain available in print as individual booklets. The walks have been tried and tested over many years and provide a comprehensive selection of different locations across Westmorland Dales. Publication in a single volume is intended to make this landscape accessible to both local and visitors alike. There are 60 walks in total covering Kirkby Stephen district, Stainmore, Orton Fells, Smardale, Ravenstonedale, northern Howgills and the Upper Eden upland of Hartley Fell, Mallerstang, Wild Boar Fell and The Clouds.

To supplement the route maps provided here the use of OS Outdoor Leisure 1:25000 map OL19 Howgill Fells & upper Eden Valley is recommended.

Author's disclaimer

Although the author had no difficulty of access on the routes described believing them to be on either access land, rights of way or permissive paths identified by the Ordnance Survey and Cumbria County Council the inclusion of the routes in this book does not imply that a right of way exists in every case and for all time. Any known problems at the time of writing have been highlighted and it remains up to the individual to make their own decision about the use of the route in each case.

Section 1
Kirkby Stephen district & Stainmore

Walk 1: Greenriggs & Croglam
Walk 2: Two Eden footbridges
Walk 3: Waitby & Greenriggs
Walk 4: Hartley & Winton
Walk 5: Stenkrith Park
Walk 6: Sandwath
Walk 7: Jubilee Nature Park & Nateby
Walk 8: Smardale, Soulby & Winton
Walk 9: Settle-Carlisle Station (KSW)
Walk 10: Kirkby Stephen Town Trail
Walk 11: The Eden Viaducts Walk
Walk 12: Waitby & Smardale Mill
Walk 13: Lockthwaite & Nateby
Walk 14: South Stainmore
Walk 15: Kirkby Stephen to Pendragon Castle
Walk 16: Kirkby Stephen Poetry Path

Pendragon Castle, Mallerstang

Walk 1: Greenriggs & Croglam

DESCRIPTION: A 2½ mile circular walk across fields returning on the Coast-to-Coast route on a good track and passing the site of an ancient earthwork - Croglam Castle. **TIME**: 1-1¼ hours. **START**: Kirkby Stephen Market Square.

From Market Square cross over Market Street and into a narrow passageway which leads to Faraday Road. A lintel bears the date 1636 and initials BG. Cross Faraday Road and continue forward on the pedestrian way with the Auction Mart on the left. After a short distance turn left over a stile to follow a waymarked path adjacent to the Mart. Briefly join some tarmac, bear right and then keep left on a green fenced path which leads to the Grammar school tennis courts - enclosed by leylandii trees. Continue straight forward to clear the tennis courts into playing fields and cross the stile into a field. Turn left and follow the wall to an ancient tree, through a gate and again follow the wall with rugby pitch on the left. Leave the field by a small waymarked gate and turn right into a green lane. To the left a track returns to Kirkby Stephen via the Westgarth estate. Continue right and after a few yards turn left over a waymarked stile and forward to cross another stile. Proceed forward and uphill to pass an old ash tree and continue forward keeping to the crest of the hill to reach a waymarked stile in the fence. Cross the stile and keep left of the barn to cross the field.

Descend towards a new barn and cross the stile before it to join the access road for Greenriggs, then turn left. Continue on this road to Faraday Road.

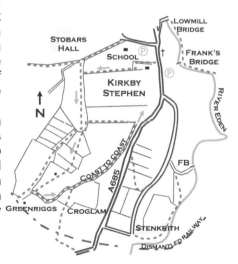

Walk 2: Two Eden Footbridges

DESCRIPTION: A 2 mile circular walk linking two Eden footbridges (Bollam and Frank's) concluding on the riverbank below Hartley village. **TIME**: 1 - 1¼ hours. **START**: Kirkby Stephen Market Square.

From Market Square head south down Market Street to pass the Tourist Information Centre. Just past Barclays Bank turn left into Little Wiend, a narrow passageway which continues down to Melbecks. At the bottom turn right and continue up Melbecks to the B6259 Nateby road. Turn left, cross the road and continue on Nateby road passing the primary school. On the outskirts of the town just beyond Bollam Cottage take the signed bridleway on the left and follow the track down to Bollam bridge. Cross the river Eden on the footbridge and continue on the bridleway to pass a ruinous barn and poetry stones. Proceed through a gate to a T-junction and turn left. This bridleway continues back to Frank's Bridge and the town first through woodland and, after crossing a small footbridge over a stream, follows the riverbank.

Continue by the river and pass left through a kissing gate to Frank's Bridge. Once over the bridge turn right to climb the steps and join Stoneshot to return to Market Square.

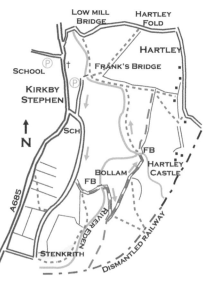

Walk 3: Waitby & Greenriggs

DESCRIPTION: A 5 mile circular walk in fields and some minor road. **TIME**: 1¾ - 2¼ hours. **START:** Kirkby Stephen Market Square.

Cross Market Street into the narrow passage with a lintel dated 1636 then cross the road and straight forward into a narrow lane adjacent to the Auction Mart.

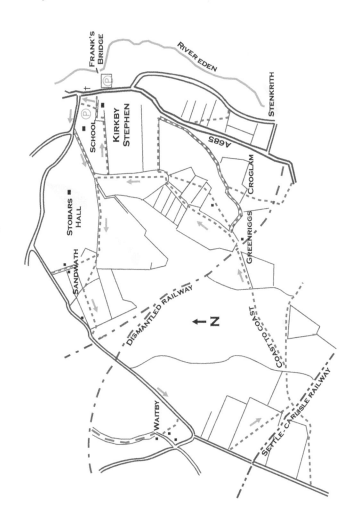

Walk 3: Waitby & Greenriggs

Turn right into the car park and cross to exit into Christian Head then turning left. To the right of the Grammar School entrance take the stile signed for Galebars and Greenriggs and then follow the sign for Stobars Lane. Keep right and take the waymarked stile at the gate. Continue straight ahead by the fence and follow this through a gate and then turn right by the waymarked stone stile. Continue forward to cross a low bridge and then diagonally across the field to cross a waymarked concrete bridge. Bear left to the field corner and cross the concrete bridge and gate. Continue straight forward to the top of the field to a stone stile and bear right to a stone stile to join a minor road and turn left. This road section is about one mile and involves taking a left turn signed for Ravenstonedale at Waitby. After the turn take the gate on the left into the third field. This is a public footpath but not signposted. Keep to the wall edge and follow a track through a sunken valley which winds gently uphill. Continue to the railway embankment and turn left through a gate. Cross the field diagonally to a stone stile. Continue forward bearing slightly left to pass a waymark through the fence and descend along an obvious path to a stile and gate in the wall. Continue to descend by the wall passing a barn to the left. Pass through the gate and straight forward under the old railway. Turn right through Greenriggs yard (or the diversion offered) and left in front of the house leaving on the farm road. Take the waymarked stile on the left and continue forward to a track and bear left. Forward through a gate and cross a further gate and, after 30 yards, a stone stile. Continue straight on by the fence onto a more obvious track, cross the stream, and straight forward to a waymark following this to the right on a bridleway. After 25 yards cross a stile and continue bearing left and through a gate into a field. Continue towards an old gatepost and take the stile on the right to enter the school grounds. Straight forward and right of the tennis courts heading towards the Auction Mart. At the perimeter of the mart turn left, crossing the stile, and turn right to join the outward route.

Walk 4: Hartley & Winton

DESCRIPTION: A 5 mile circular walk to Hartley and then a section of the dismantled Stainmore railway. The route returns across fields to the village of Winton. **TIME**: 2 - 2¼ hours. **START:** Kirkby Stephen Market Square.

Proceed east and descend Stoneshot to Frank's Bridge. Cross the footbridge and turn immediately left to traverse right, around the cricket field. Pass through a gate and continue forward to cross the stream, join the road turning right to Hartley.

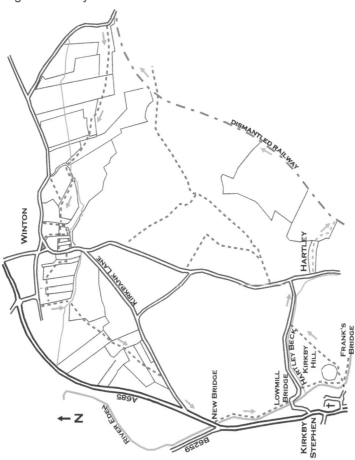

Walk 4: Hartley & Winton

Enter the village of Hartley and at the T junction turn right. Turn left through a gate at the plaque for *John Strutt Conservation Foundation*. Follow the track uphill, through a field gate and continue to the gate beside the dismantled railway. Join the line and continue left along the railway for about one mile. Join the road, turn left and after 200m left into a field signed for Winton. Continue forward on a green track and cross a stile in the wall about 100m below a gate. Again continue forward, cross another stile and bear right towards a wall and cross a wall stile. Bear left to a young tree plantation and cross a stile in the field corner on the right. Turn left and immediately cross another stile to continue downhill towards a stream. Cross the stream by a low bridge and bear left to cross a stile in the field corner. Turn left and after a short distance cross a stile on the right. Turn left and forward to cross a stile and bear right uphill - ignore a stile on the right - continuing straight forward and pass through two field gates and then, in quick succession, five stiles. Go down the steps and join the road, turn right into the village of Winton. At the Bay Horse Inn turn left, left again and straight forward on the road. Bear left as the main road swings right and then turn left to follow a pathway signed *Eden Place*. Cross a stile into a field and follow the trees down hill crossing a stile and footbridge in a wall. Cross the lower part of the field to a stile in a single piece of wall. Keep left on the field edge and then straight forward to cross a stile by a sycamore tree. Keep left to the field edge, cross a stile and continue straight forward to cross a stile. Continue diagonally across the field and cross a stile on left. Again cross this field diagonally to the stile and join a minor road. Turn right to join the A685 Brough - Kirkby Stephen road and continue left towards Kirkby Stephen on a good pavement. Just before the bridge take the path left signed *Low Mill Bridge*. Follow the riverside path to Low Mill, turn left at the road and take the path on the right signed *Hartley & Nateby* crossing a footbridge to the cricket field. Keep right on the perimeter of this field to reach Frank's Bridge.

Walk 5: Stenkrith Park

DESCRIPTION: A 3 mile circular walk to the attractive riverside of Stenkrith Park returning on the dismantled Stainmore railway. **TIME**: 1 - 1½ hours. **START**: Kirkby Stephen Market Square.

Head south down Market Street to pass the Tourist Information Centre. Just past Barclays Bank turn left into Little Wiend, a narrow passageway which continues down to Melbecks. At Melbecks turn right and continue up Melbecks to the B6259 Nateby road. Turn left, cross the road and continue on Nateby road passing the primary school. On the outskirts of the town just beyond Bollam Cottage take the signed bridleway on the left and follow the track down to enter the field at the first gate. Bear right below the old hawthorns and diagonally down to the river Eden. Pass through a gate and continue forward on the riverside. Enter Stenkrith Park at the stile/gate and continue on the track through woodland. Follow the track out towards Nateby road but do not leave Stenkrith. Turn left and cross the Millennium footbridge. Again turn left and continue forward on the dismantled railway for about ¼ mile and turn right to leave the line just before the first bridge. Pass through a gate and left to join another bridleway

and cross the bridge. Follow this ancient high-banked track and cross the small footbridge continuing uphill. Take the right hand track when the path forks. This bridleway continues back to Frank's bridge first through woodland and, after crossing a footbridge, the path follows the riverbank. Pass through a kissing gate and left to Frank's bridge. Once over the bridge turn right to the steps and join Stoneshot to Market Square.

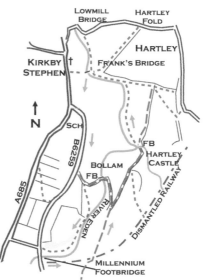

DESCRIPTION: A short, peaceful 2½ mile circular walk **on** bridleways and public footpaths. **TIME**: 1-1¼ hours. **START**: Kirkby Stephen Market Square.

From the Market Square cross Market Street and enter the narrow passageway with a lintel dated 1636. At Faraday road turn right and go straight forward at the staggered junction into Redmayne Road. Just past the Coop follow the concrete road signed; *Greensike Lane.* Pass the cemetery and continue forward into an enclosed lane. At the T junction turn left and continue forward to pass a modern barn on left. At the minor road (for Soulby) turn right and after 60 yards turn left signed: *Sandwath Bridge.* At the next minor road Kirkby Stephen electricity substation is on the left. The remains of the old Sandwath bridge and ford are adjacent to the new. Turn right and then take the left fork for Waitby. Continue up the narrow lane and turn left on the farm access road signed for Kirkby Stephen. Pass through the farm and two gates to enter a field. Keep on the track, cross a stream and as the track divides go straight forward to a wall stile in the field corner. Turn left and continue uphill between fences, pass through a gate and straight forward on the field edge down to a gate/stile. Turn immediately right through a small gate signed *Tarn Lane.* Keep to the field edge and take the stile to the left to enter the school playing fields. Go straight forward keeping the tennis courts on the left and head towards the Auction Mart. At the perimeter of the mart turn left by cattle pens. Cross the stile, turn right down a narrow lane to Faraday Road to join the outward route.

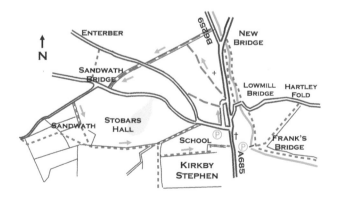

Walk 7: Jubilee Nature Park & Nateby

DESCRIPTION: A 5½ mile circular walk visiting Jubilee Nature Park and passing close to Wharton Hall returning through Nateby village. Return by old bridleways and riverside. **TIME**: 2-2¼ hours. **START**: Kirkby Stephen Market Square.

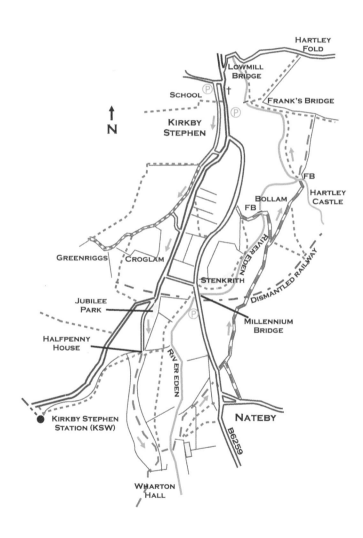

Walk 7: Jubilee Nature Park & Nateby

From Market Square cross Market Street and enter the narrow passage with the inscription 1636 on the lintel. At Faraday Road turn left and continue up the road. After about ½ mile the road is unmade and passes garages. Keep straight on for another ½ mile. This track continues on to Greenriggs - encountered on Walk 1 - but bear left in front of the last house to enter a small housing estate. Follow the road bearing to the right and then left into Rowgate. At the main road turn right and continue up South Road. Take care and cross the main road just before the road bridge to take the pedestrian route across the bridge. Ahead is Jubilee Nature Park. Pass through the gates to walk uphill to the new summerhouse. Bear right and exit the park by the top gate. Join the road and turn left to continue towards Wharton Hall. Pass over the cattle grid at Halfpenny House and continue down the concrete road. Continue down the road, cross the cattle grid and after 200 yards pass through the gate signed for Nateby. Ahead is Wharton Hall, once the seat of the Wharton family, and now a private house. Walk straight downhill to cross the bridge, turn left and pass through a gate at the next field boundary. Keep by the riverbank for a short distance and then follow the bridleway as it traverses gently uphill away from the river. Pass through a gate and continue straight forward on the fence side to another gate at the northern end of the village which gives access to the B6259. Turn left on the road and after 75 yards turn right signed public bridleway. Follow this for ¼ mile to a gate adjacent to the dismantled Stainmore railway line. Continue forward on the same track and cross the bridge over the former railway. Follow this ancient high-banked track - which can be muddy. Cross the small footbridge and continue gently uphill. Take the right hand track when the path forks, this bridleway continues back to Frank's bridge and the town, first through woodland and, after crossing a footbridge, the path follows the riverbank. Follow the river, pass through a kissing gate and on to Frank's bridge. Once over the bridge turn right to the steps and join Stoneshot to return to Market Square.

DESCRIPTION: A moderate 8 mile circular walk passing through Soulby and Winton. **TIME**: 3 - 4 hours. **START**: Kirkby Stephen Market Square. Route map o/leaf.

Cross Market Street into the passage with a lintel dated 1636. Cross the road and straight forward into a narrow lane adjacent to the Auction Mart. Turn right into the car park and cross to exit onto the road turning left. To the right of the Grammar School entrance take the stile signed for *Galebars and Greenriggs*. Pass the Sports Pavilion on the left and follow the sign for *Stobars Lane*. Keep right and take the waymarked stile at the gate. Continue straight ahead by the fence and follow this down through a gate and then turn right by the waymarked stone stile. Continue forward to cross a low waymarked bridge and then diagonally across the field to cross a waymarked concrete bridge. Bear left to the field corner and cross the concrete bridge and gate. Continue straight forward to the top of the field to a waymarked stone stile, bear right to a stone stile to join a minor road. Turn left up the steep hill and cross two bridges over the dismantled railways. Immediately after the second bridge turn right through a gate signed *DEFRA Conservation Walk*. Descend to the track and turn left. Continue forward and briefly leave the line to cross a track and a minor road. Just before this section terminates at Smardale turn right through a gate and left up the road. At the junction turn right signed for *Crosby Garrett: Narrow road and ford.* Follow the road down, cross the footbridge and turn right to cross a stile into a field next to the river. Continue forward to cross three fields and take the footbridge over the Scandal beck bearing left to pass through the yard at Smardale Mill. Join the minor road, turn left up a steep hill and take the track on the left as the road swings to the right. Follow this track to Leases and continue forward to the left of the buildings to follow the river. Continue forward bearing right and eventually re-join the riverbank and an obvious track which climbs to a gate. Cross the field to the right of the barn and join the road. Turn left and left again to Soulby. Cross the bridge and at the crossroads turn right down the road. After ½ mile turn right signed *Public By-road Winton.* Follow this road for about 1½ miles crossing a dismantled railway and the river Eden and join the Appleby Road at Beckfoot. Continue forward down Daleholme Lane - a narrow minor road. At the A685 cross the road into Winton and as the road bears left turn right signed as a no through road and then turn left to follow a pathway signed *Eden Place.*

Walk 8: Smardale, Soulby & Winton

Cross a stile and follow the trees down hill crossing a stile and footbridge in a wall. Cross the lower part of the field to a stile in a single piece of wall. Keep left on the field edge and then straight forward to a stile by a sycamore tree. Keep left to the field edge, cross a stile and continue straight forward to cross a stile. Continue diagonally across the field and cross a stile on left. Again cross this field diagonally and join the minor road. Turn right to join the A685 Brough - Kirkby Stephen road and continue left towards Kirkby Stephen on a good pavement. Just before the bridge take the path left signed *Low Mill Bridge.* Follow the riverside path to Low Mill, turn left at the road and take the path on the right signed *Hartley & Nateby* crossing a footbridge to the cricket field. Keep right on the perimeter of this field to reach Frank's Bridge. Cross the bridge and turn immediately right to Stoneshot and Market Square.

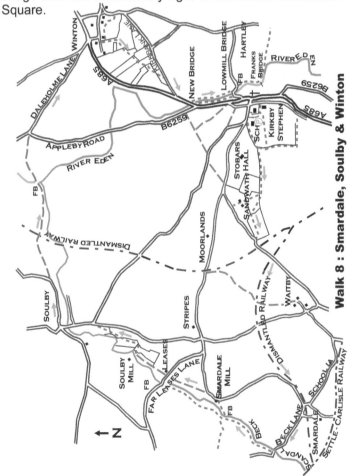

Walk 8 : Smardale, Soulby & Winton

Walk 9: Settle-Carlisle Station, Kirkby Stephen

DESCRIPTION: A linear 2½ mile walk to the station avoiding the busy A685 **TIME**: 45 mins - 1 hour. **START**: Kirkby Stephen Market Square.

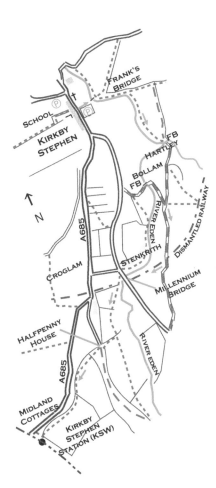

Walk east away from the church and follow Stoneshot down to Frank's Bridge. Cross the bridge, turn right and follow the river Eden. After the kissing gate turn right and continue to follow the riverbank south. After a gate and footbridge continue into a wooded section and follow this bridleway for approx ½ mile. The track crosses a bridge over the dismantled Stainmore railway. Just after the bridge turn right to join the old railway line. Bear left for a few hundred yards and cross the river Eden on the Millennium footbridge at Stenkrith. Follow the path out to the B6259 and turn left on the road. Just before the bridge turn right through a gate to descend steps and continue along the riverbank. After the dismantled bridge turn sharp right, cross the stile into a field and continue uphill. Take another stile and continue on the riverbank uphill to a wall stile. Cross this stile turning right to follow the field edge to Halfpenny House. Cross the road and join the tarmac path which proceeds directly to the station.

Walk 10: Kirkby Stephen Town Trail

DESCRIPTION: An easy circular walk visiting some familiar landmarks around the town. **TIME**: 1 hour. **START**: Market Square.

In Market Square the circle of cobbles defines an area used, at one time, for bull baiting. The Cloisters, and their eight Tuscan columns, were built in 1810 to act as a screen for the church entrance. To start the brief tour of the town bear right away from the Cloisters and at the car park turn left into Vicarage Lane. The road narrows and passes the old Grammar School endowed by Thomas, first Lord Wharton in 1561. Continue to bear left down to the main road, turn left back towards the town and left again up steps into Church Walk. Turn left through the gate into the churchyard and the parish church of St. Stephen. It is an old church with traces of Saxon and Norman work. Inside there are various antiquities including the Loki stone or "bound devil" with both Norse and pagan associations. Continue out through the Cloisters and forward into Market Street. Just past Barclays Bank turn left into Little Wiend - a narrow defensive passageway - then right through an archway into Royal Arcade. Cross the cobbles diagonally and return to Market Street. The bank on the left, one of the best buildings in Kirkby Stephen, still retains the original Martin's Bank deposit box. The facade was built in 1903. Continue along Market Street to the traffic lights and notice an original iron signpost in miles and furlongs! Ahead the main road narrows, another indicator of a defensive role at the original limits of the medieval town. Turn left at the traffic lights and pass the eccentric Temperance Hall built in 1856. To the right is Victoria Square and the old site for the Post Office. Pass the Temperance Hall and left into Mellbecks and continue forward passing the Manor House on the right. The road continues to Frank's bridge and the site of an old brewery. The footbridge dates back to the sixteenth century. Once over the footbridge there are footpaths to Low Mill, Hartley and, on the riverside, Stenkrith Park, Nateby and Wharton. Finish by turning left before Frank's bridge into Stoneshot, a walled lane, which returns to Market Square.

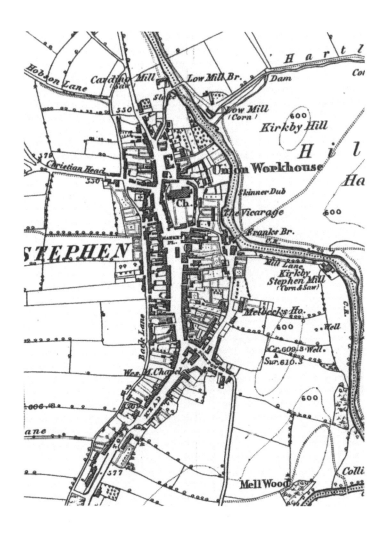

*Kirkby Stephen town from the first edition 6 inch to one mile
Ordnance Survey map, 1862.*

Walk 11: The Eden Viaducts Walk

DESCRIPTION: A 4 mile circular walk staying close to the banks of the river Eden and connecting with the dismantled Stainmore railway at Stenkrith Park. **TIME**: 1½ - 2 hours.
START: Kirkby Stephen Market Square.

From Market Square proceed east in front of The Cloisters and pass into Stoneshot to Frank's Bridge. Cross the bridge turning right to follow the river. After the kissing gate turn right to continue on the river bank. Pass over the gated footbridge and continue on the bridleway. Take the right fork in the path down a hedged lane to cross the river by a footbridge at Bollam. Turn left and continue upstream into Stenkrith Park. The path winds up to Nateby road but turn left within the park to cross the Millennium footbridge. Turn left onto the dismantled Stainmore railway track and continue forward to cross Podgill and Merrygill Viaducts. This permissive route terminates at Hartley Quarry at which point turn left down the

road. A short cut on the left just past Beech House avoids using a narrow section of road. Back on the road turn left over a narrow footbridge and proceed into Hartley turning left into a lane in front of Saltpie Hall. This path returns to join the outward route.

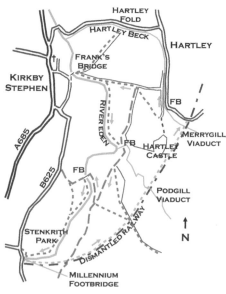

Walk 12: Waitby & Smardale Mill

DESCRIPTION: A 3 mile circular walk on part of the dismantled Stainmore railway. The first part is on a concessionary right of way by DEFRA and then follows the Scandal Beck to Smardale Mill returning by minor road, bridleway and old railway. **TIME**: 1½ - 2 hours. **START**: Limited parking at NY756086 approx 1 mile west of Kirkby Stephen.

From Kirkby Stephen take the road to Soulby and turn left just past the Grammar School signed for Smardale. Follow this road as it narrows and climbs steeply, park just beyond the second bridge. Access the former rail track through the gate descending to the line. Turn left until the path descends to cross a farm track at a dismantled bridge. Cross and continue on the railway to another dismantled bridge to cross a road. Again continue on the line through a cutting and leave at a gate adjacent to a minor road. Turn left on the road and bear right by the former station house. Follow the road and cross the footbridge over Scandal Beck turning right to follow the beck and cross the footbridge over it. Bear left to Smardale Mill and take the gate through the farmyard. Turn left at the road and uphill to pass Stripes Farm. At Waitby Crossing turn right on the bridleway in front of the old station house. Follow to reach the outward route for the return.

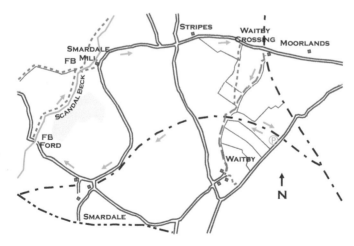

Walk 13: Lockthwaite & Nateby

DESCRIPTION: A 3½ mile circular walk starting from Kirkby Stephen. Crossing the dismantled Stainmore railway the route crosses pasture returning through Nateby village.

TIME: 1½ - 2 hours. **START:** Kirkby Stephen Market Square.
Take the outgoing route of Walk 51 Ewbank Scar and after crossing the old railway continue uphill to cross two stiles. Cross at the third stile to turn right passing an old barn. Follow the bridleway uphill and pass through a gate on the right, it is tucked out of site behind piles of stone. Signposting is also minimal at this point. Proceed forward diagonally across the field and aim to arrive in front of and below Lockthwaite then bearing right to follow a field wall on the left. Pass through a gate and two fields before crossing a stile through the wall and descend to the B6270. Turn right to descend into Nateby village and bear right at the beck to join a well defined bridleway which leads back to the Stainmore railway track. Pass through a gate to join the line turning left to cross the river Eden on the Millennium footbridge. Bear right to follow the river downstream through Stenkrith Park. Continue down river and as Bollam footbridge comes into view bear left through a gate to join an obvious track that leads out to the B6259 for the return

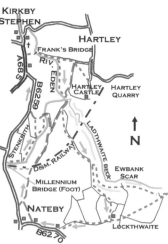

Bollam footbridge

Walk 14: South Stainmore (South Section)

DESCRIPTION: A 7½ mile circular walk starting from Barras visiting the site of Belah Viaduct on the dismantled Stainmore railway and Argill Woods. **TIME**: 4½ hours. **START**: Lay-by at Barras grid NY836121. The route can easily be divided into two separate walks.

From the lay-by walk down the road to the former chapel (Mouthlock Centre) at the South Stainmore crossroads and take the minor no through road south. Cross the cattle grid and continue gently down hill. The road becomes unfenced, crosses through a gate and over a stream. Bear right to follow the footpath sign. This farm track terminates at Oakbank. At the farm go straight ahead to the right of the house and a barn. There is a substantial footbridge which crosses the river Belah in the valley.....

...below but there is little evidence of a path to it although the path is signed to the right of the outbuilding at Oakbank. Descend steeply from the outbuilding bearing left down an overgrown section. At the bottom proceed forward to just right of the telegraph pole over some rough ground to reach the wooden footbridge. This is a delightful and secluded wooded valley. Cross the footbridge and turn right by the river to pass through a gate. After 30 metres ascend left up a grassy bank to join a fenced track and follow it left as it zig zags uphill to the left of the fence. At the top aim for the telegraph pole in the middle of the field and continue forward to cross a stile in the fence. After the stile continue uphill onto a disused track and follow it to a gate, crossing the stile and continuing forward in the same direction.

Cross a stile in the fence ahead and descend to the tin roofed barn and keep to the left to cross a river bridge. Proceed straight up the hill keeping the fence to the right and below the farm. At the fence/wall intersection go through the gate and turn right and up to the road following it uphill between the outbuildings. At the footpath sign turn right again uphill to pass between two walls and through a gate. Continue forward on a green track towards the viaduct, pass through another gate and bear left uphill to cross the stone stile to gain access onto the dismantled rail track bed and the eastern pier of the viaduct. Cross the former railway line and proceed diagonally uphill on a small path leading to a gate in the wall. Pass through the gate and bear left to join a faint path to join up with the road. Proceed down the road and turn right through the gate to follow the public bridleway. The bridleway climbs and swings slightly right until the gradient lessens and then turn left to traverse the edge with excellent views north across the Eden valley. Join the road beyond the gate and turn left to descend to the footpath sign turning right through a stone stile and immediately left to cross another stile. Turn right and pass left of the barn and proceed forward to Barras Farm. Go through the gate and left in front of the house and as the service road turns left take the gate on the right and cross down the field to a barn. To the left of the barn cross over a broken wall on a small path and keep to the left of the stream descending to the stile in the wall and onto the road at Mousegill Low Bridge. At the road turn right uphill over Mousegill Low Bridge and turn left through the gate signed *Public footpath*. Proceed under the former railway and immediately right over a stone stile.

Walk 14: South Stainmore (North Section)

Continue forward maintaining height to join a broken wall keeping to its right. Bear right to pass through a gate immediately right over a stone stile. Continue forward maintaining height to join a broken wall keeping to its right. Bear right to pass through a gate immediately in front of Mouthlock House. Keep just left of the house and exit the enclosure through a small gate adjacent to the property, continuing forward to a track. Turn left onto the track in front of another house and carry on down to Mousegill. Pass through the gate and forward between house and outbuildings to follow the fenced grassy path to a wooden stile. Cross the stile and bear right by the fence to pass over a stone stile. Continue forward and keep the stone wall to the left in view. There is not much of a path but another stone stile is encountered quite soon.

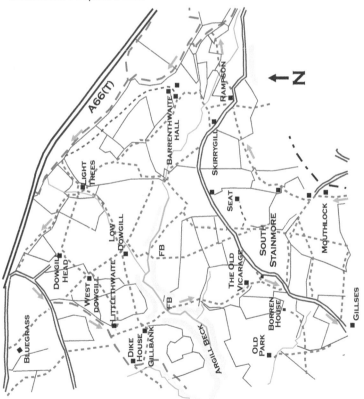

After crossing this stile keep to the same line and descend to the road at Rampson. Note the initials and date (1630) on this fine building although the present house is a little more recent. At the road turn right and pass through the gate. Once the buildings are cleared bear left off the road and down the grass slope at about 45°. This old track descends down to a quaint packhorse bridge over the stream. Once over the bridge follow an obvious track uphill, cross another field and continue towards a field barn. Keep to the right of the barn and pass through a gate at the barn side, clear the enclosed area and climb steeply uphill to a stone stile in the wall above. This stile gives access onto the Slapestone bridleway.

Keep above the wall and just before the next wall and gate bear right uphill to pass through another gate on the wall above. Turn left and continue above the wall where the old bridleway is still visible. Continue through another gate passing above Barrenthwaite Hall and climb steeply by the wall side. Follow the wall as it turns left onto a fine high level section parallel to the A66 road. Follow the wall and at the two sycamore trees the concrete road from Barrenthwaite joins the bridleway. Turn left here through a gate to descend the zig zag track to Light Trees. At the farm track turn right and follow the unmade road up to the minor road. This minor road runs west to Limes Head and follows the course of a Roman road. Turn left down this road for about ¼ mile and take the second turn left signed *Public Bridleway Argill Beck*. The unmade road swings sharp left just before a gate and follow this down hill to pass Littlethwaite and continue down the track to Gillbank. Just before the house take the stile on the left into Argill Woods (Cumbria Wildlife Trust Nature Reserve). Take the main path straight forward and continue down through the ancient woodland to cross another gate/stile and the footbridge over the stream. After crossing the footbridge the path is indistinct but continue forward on more or less the same line to climb the hill side diagonally. At the top of the slope and ahead there is a broken wall and follow this left to the stile. Cross the stile and the stream at the head of a gully and continue forward to follow the fence on the right. Pass a field barn and continue towards the Old Vicarage but aim for the edge of the trees on the right rather than taking the track into the farm. Cross the stile in the trees to follow a narrow path which skirts to the right of the farm buildings. Turn right on the unmade road to reach the minor road and then turn right on the path signed South Stainmore to reach the church. From the church continue on the road to Mouthlock and the finish of the walk.

Walk 15: Kirkby Stephen to Pendragon Castle

DESCRIPTION: A 10 mile route tracking the Eden river south on public paths, bridleways and minor roads. A shorter 6 mile route returns from Lammerside Castle. **TIME**: 4 - 5 hours or 3 - 4 hours. **START**: Kirkby Stephen Market Square.

From Market Square go towards the parish church bearing right to pass the public conveniences and follow the sign for River Eden Frank's Bridge into Stoneshot - a narrow, high-walled lane. Again follow the sign for Frank's Bridge left down a few steps and then left to cross Frank's Bridge to follow the path right and upstream. Shortly the path reaches a gate to enter a field. Turn right to follow the sign for Podgill by the tree lined river Eden.

At the field end cross the narrow, gated footbridge and continue on the ancient bridleway through woodland. The path narrows between two fields but keep straight on ignoring another path joining from the right. Cross a small stream on a narrow bridge and climb gently through more trees. Emerging from the trees the track crosses a bridge over the dismantled railway and swings right. Turn right through the wide gate to join the former railway line turning left to walk along an impressive wooded embankment. Cross the Millennium Bridge to your right. From the Millennium Bridge follow the approach path out to access the B6259 Kirkby Stephen to Nateby road.Turn left and before crossing the road bridge take the steps down on the right with the footpath signed for Wharton. Follow the path by the river negotiating more steps down and bearing right by the foundations of the old railway bridge. Take the gate into the field and continue on the path up the field by the river. At the top of the field turn right after a wall stile and proceed straight forward to Halfpenny House.

At Halfpenny pass through the gate and cross the road that leads south to Wharton Hall and continue on the tarmac cycle path up the wall side to Kirkby Stephen railway station. From the field gate turn right down the concourse to join the A685, turn left to continue up the road and at the first junction turn left on the A683 Sedbergh road and left again on the minor road signed for Wharton Dykes.

Walk 15: Kirkby Stephen to Pendragon Castle

The minor road can be used as far as Lammerside Castle (about one mile). As Croop House is approached the road swings right and down hill but continue to follow the wall on the left. A choice of route is available here with the longer option continuing to Pendragon. If a look at Lammerside is required or the shorter six mile option then turn left through the gate to the ruin.

To continue on the main route to Pendragon Castle return to the gate from Lammerside turning left to pass immediately through another gate to join the bridleway which skirts the base of Birkett Common. After about 1½ miles the track joins the *Tommy Road.* Turn left over the cattle grid and down the narrow road to the bridge. Just over the bridge there is a footpath sign left which is the route to be followed - but not before visiting Pendragon Castle just a short walk up the road. Until now the castle has been invisible and it is a surprise to discover this picturesque ruin set on the bank of the river Eden.

From Pendragon return to Castle bridge and take the footpath on the right crossing two further stiles and keeping left of Moorriggs to join the B6259. Turn left onto the road and then take the footpath signed for Nateby on the right after a few hundred yards at Southwaite. Pass between the two houses and through the gate to bear slightly right uphill to pass through the gate at the top. Turn left and traverse through fields crossing a beck and stile towards Carr House. Pass above Carr House and cross the stream to join an old track through woodland. At the edge of the woods cross the stile through the wall as it angles and continue on the track above the wall on the lower fellside. The track continues above Dalefoot and is indistinct in places but as the wall drops to the road keep at roughly the same height and contour parallel with the road.

Lammerside Castle on the bank of the Eden river

Walk 15: Kirkby Stephen to Pendragon Castle

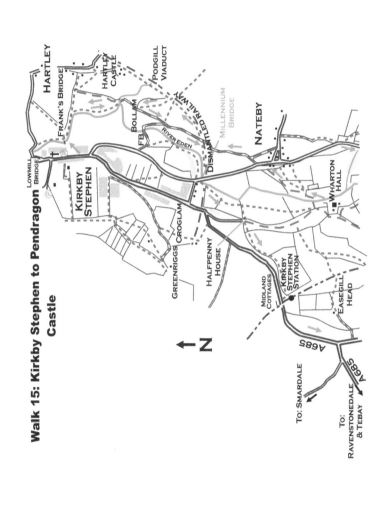

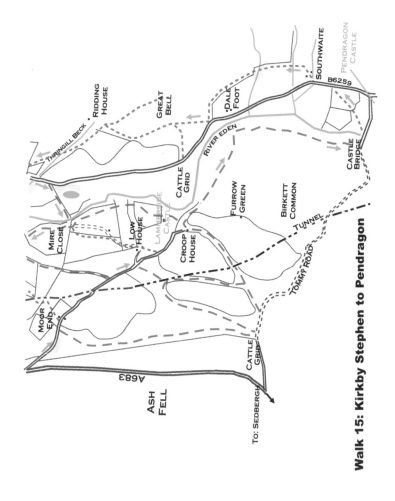

Walk 15: Kirkby Stephen to Pendragon

Walk 15: Kirkby Stephen to Pendragon Castle

Shortly another wall rises from the left from the road and stay with this wall to Thringill Beck. The ruin of Ridding House will come into view. At the beck cross the stile on the left and follow the beck down hill by the line of a broken wall. The path is not obvious here but continue to descend by the broken wall and cross at the gated fence continuing with the dry beck on the right. Shortly the path crosses the beck at a footbridge. Take the garden style gate and continue forward by the telegraph pole and through two more field gates keeping to the outside of the boundary wall of Thringill. Continue forward to join the B6259 just south of Nateby village.

Turn left and take the road south for ¼ mile and the bridleway right signed for Wharton. The bridleway crosses over Mire Close bridge at which point turn right for Wharton Hall. On reaching Wharton Hall turn left up the concrete track and right through a gate into the field, proceed forward to another gate and then gently descend to the old oak tree and signposts at the concrete road at the other side of the Hall. Cross the access road to follow the bridleway signed for Nateby. Cross the river Eden at the wooden bridge and follow the river left to pass through another gate. The path slowly starts to climb away from the river, through another gate. Follow the fence line straight on to another gate to the left of the end house of Nateby village.

At the B6259 turn left and immediately right to follow the bridleway for Kirkby Stephen. Cross the stream and continue on the bridleway and then left through the gate encountered on the outward journey to gain access onto the dismantled railway at Stenkrith. Turn right this time to follow the old line passing through two gates. At the next bridge over the old railway line the return route branches left up the embankment. Through the gate continue forward on a vague path which runs parallel with the wall. As the wall swings away right continue straight on to descend to the field corner and gate accessing the bridleway used on the outward journey. Turn right to return to Kirkby Stephen by the same route as the outward journey

Walk 16: Kirkby Stephen Poetry Path

DESCRIPTION: An easy 3½ walk on public footpaths, bridleways and permissive routes tracking close to the banks of the Eden river just south of Kirkby Stephen town. **TIME:** 1 - 1½ hours. **START:** Kirkby Stephen Market Square.

Use the outward routes described in Walks 5 and 11 to Bollam or Frank's Bridge to start on Poetry Path. The sculptures (No. 1 - 12) run clockwise on either bank of the Eden river with the return through Stenkrith Park.

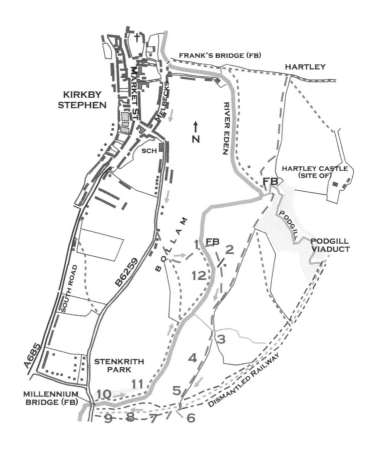

Section 2
Orton Fells & Smardale

Location Map for Walks 17 - 26 overleaf
Walk 17: Smardale Gill & Smardale Fell
Walk 18: Great Asby Scar & Castle Folds
Walk 19: Potts Valley & Little Asby Scar
Walk 20: Nettle Hill & Ladle Lane
Walk 21: Crosby Ravensworth Fell
Walk 22: Orton Scar & Knott
Walk 23: Ash Fell Edge
Walk 24: Great Ewe Fell
Walk 25: Oddendale & Hardendale
Walk 26: Great & Little Kinmond

Note: Walks 28 and 32 for Smardale and Walk 31 Ash Fell are in Section 3 Ravenstonedale & Northern Howgills.

Below: Potts Valley

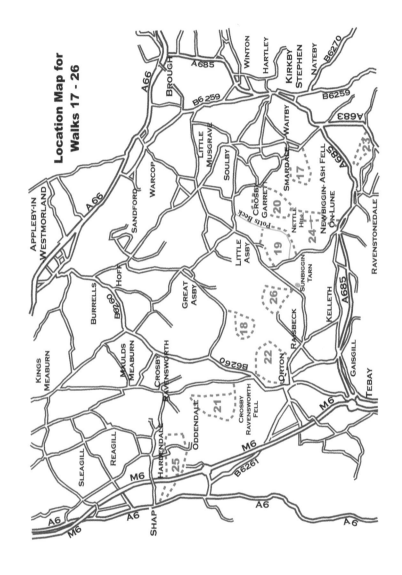

Location Map for
Walks 17 - 26

Walk 17: Smardale Gill & Smardale Fell

DESCRIPTION: A 6 mile circular walk onto Smardale Gill Nature Reserve on a dismantled section of the Stainmore railway. The route then connects with Wainwright's Coast-to-Coast walk for the return across Smardale Fell. **TIME:** 2 - 2½ hours. **START:** At Smardale Gill Nature Reserve car park Limited roadside parking is also available in the vicinity of NY747073.

From the car park join the dismantled railway to enter the Nature Reserve. The Settle-Carlisle line passes overhead at Smardale Viaduct and the old line continues in a spectacular traverse high above Scandal Beck emerging to cross the beck on another impressive viaduct at Smardalegill.

Do not cross the viaduct instead take the permissive route that continues (leaving the railway) to the left and traverses an old quarry route to Smardale Bridge.

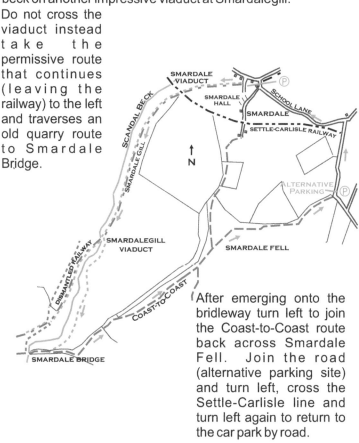

After emerging onto the bridleway turn left to join the Coast-to-Coast route back across Smardale Fell. Join the road (alternative parking site) and turn left, cross the Settle-Carlisle line and turn left again to return to the car park by road.

Walk 18: Great Asby Scar & Castle Folds

DESCRIPTION: A 5½ mile circular walk passing through Great Asby National Nature Reserve including the fortified knoll known as Castle Folds which is possibly pre-Roman. Mainly on bridleways and paths although the approach to Castle Folds requires some care to navigate through the limestone pavement. *The nature reserve is set in a unique upland landscape of limestone outcrops with exceptional views across the Eden valley.* **TIME:** 2 hours. **START:** On the minor road 2 miles SW of Great Asby village. Grid NY664115. The walk can be started at Great Asby taking the minor road to Copper Mines Lane.

Follow the bridleway signed as Copper Mines Lane. Just before the first access gate to open fell there is a mine entrance in the field on the right. Pass through the first gate and continue forward to enter the Nature Reserve ahead. Leave the bridleway and follow a faint path next to the wall on the left. After about ½ mile cross the wall stile and continue uphill next to the wall and then trend left towards the limestone pavement. The pavement can be avoided by traversing round to the left. The knoll of Castle Folds is the obvious elevated platform.

Leave on its southern edge where a route can be negotiated and aim for the wall corner where another ladder stile permits access back over the wall. Follow the wall and rejoin the bridleway turning right to cross the reserve. Pass a disused quarry on the right and follow the waymarked sign to return to the point of entry and retrace the outward route.

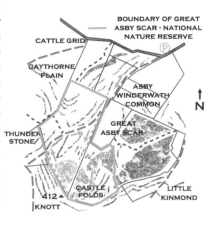

BOUNDARY OF GREAT ASBY SCAR - NATIONAL NATURE RESERVE

CATTLE GRID

GAYTHORNE PLAIN

ASBY WINDERWATH COMMON

N

GREAT ASBY SCAR

THUNDER STONE

CASTLE FOLDS

412 KNOTT

LITTLE KINMOND

Walk 19: Potts Valley & Little Asby Scar

DESCRIPTION: A six mile circular walk taking in the quiet charm of Potts Valley followed by a short steep ascent to reach the tiny village of Little Asby. The route continues onto Little Asby Common - an SSI and conservation area - with limestone outcropping. The limestone can be easily navigated for the return to the start point. **TIME:** 2 - 2½ hours. **START:** Off the unfenced road at NY 686091.

From Middle Busk follow the unfenced road down to pass the houses at Mazon Wath and Fell Head. Immediately after Fell Head turn left at the footpath sign and follow the track towards Potts Valley. Keep above the enclosure wall and then bear left on an obvious path towards Potts Beck passing through a gate. Continue down the valley passing through two gates in quick succession to the ruined farm of Potts. Turn left over the footbridge, cross the stile and head straight uphill adjacent to the wall. Continue over further stiles to gain access into a walled lane which leads into Little Asby. Turn left onto the metalled road and continue straight through Little Asby. At the top of the village pass through a gate onto the common. Follow a track by the wall until it starts to swing away right continuing forward to find a route through the limestone pavement back to the start.

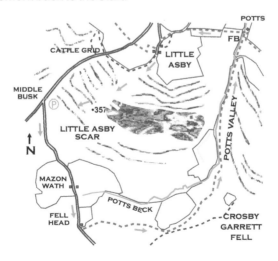

Walk 20: Nettle Hill & Ladle Lane

DESCRIPTION:An easy 4½ mile circular with an ascent to Nettle Hill (382m) on Crosby Garrett Fell returning on a public bridleway and footpaths. **TIME**: 1½ - 2 hours. **START**: Crosby Garrett village - parking adjacent to the railway viaduct.

Cross under the Settle-Carlisle railway viaduct and join the public bridleway for Brownber. After about ¼ mile a track bears off right onto the fell side and develops into an obvious banked trackway which climbs gently to Beacon Hill. From Beacon Hill bear right across open ground to attain the trig point on Nettle Hill. From Nettle Hill bear west to join the public bridleway - there is a waymark post at the point where the bridleway forks. Take the left hand fork and continue north to Windy Bank and stay on the left hand path at the next waymark post and enter the walled lane of Newclose Lane at the fell gate. Continue down the lane and turn right through a gate signed *Public Bridleway Crosby Garrett.* Cross two fields and enter Ladle Lane at the gate and turn left to follow the lane down to Crosby Garrett. Continue down Ladle Lane and cross the railway line at the former Station House to return.

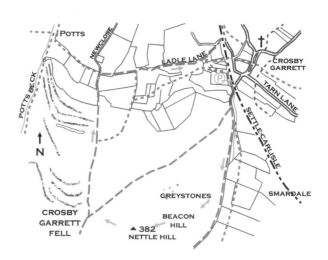

Walk 21: Crosby Ravensworth Fell

DESCRIPTION: A 7½ mile circular walk starting on the Coast-to-Coast route and skirting the perimeter of a medieval deer park. The walk then heads north returning through fields passing Crosby Lodge to rejoin the outward route. **TIME**: 2½ - 3 hours **START**: Roadside 3½ miles south of Crosby Ravensworth at NY626111.

Cross the fence stile and continue on an obvious waymarked track which meets the deer wall boundary after about ½ mile. Continue to track the wall crossing two steep gills. At a section of re-built wall the wall swings sharp right and the path ahead can be seen traversing up hill adjacent to two large boulders. At the large boulder bear right to the wall corner and continue north following the wall until it joins the main bridleway then continue forward for another two miles. Bear right to follow the right hand wall and connect to the footpath passing into the field to start the return journey. Keep forward to pass through a double gate and forward again to a gated fence. At the field corner continue forward again bearing slightly left to descend to the beck and the second footbridge.

Cross the bridge/stile and diagonally uphill to a wall stile and then a gate just below Crosby Lodge. Keep forward again to join a field track and leave the track as it bears right just before the next fence. Continue into the field and bear gently right to join the fence. At the boundary wall pass through the gate to access the stile and return on the outward route.

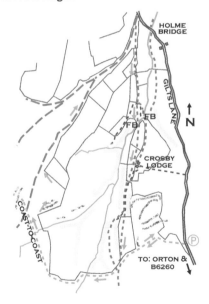

DESCRIPTION: A 5½ mile circular walk to Beacon Hill continuing through limestone pavement to Knott. **TIME**: 2½ - 3 hours. **START**: Orton village hall.

Go north on the B6260 Appleby road and turn right over a small road bridge to pass in front of The Old Vicarage. Just before the next bridge turn left into the No Through Road at the bridleway sign. Turn left at the next bridleway sign for Broadfell which passes between houses into a narrow enclosed lane. Continue on this gated track joining a beck to the right and then cross the beck over a small bridge and continue forward into Broadfell by a gate to the left of a barn. Exit the yard through another gate continuing uphill towards a wood. Pass through another gate and uphill by the wood to a limekiln. After another gate join the B6260. Turn right on the road and immediately right after the cattle grid onto open ground above the fell wall. Follow the wall edge to reach Monument and continue forward to track the wall and join the bridleway, pass right through the gate and descend on the bridleway to a footpath sign. Pass through the next gate and continue to descend to a piece of outcropping limestone and then bear left onto open ground and continue uphill through the limestone pavement aiming for the trig point on the wall edge. To continue descend roughly south west to three cairns and then pick a route through the limestone to rejoin the bridleway adjacent to a reservoir and the fell wall. Turn left on the bridleway, through a gate into Knott Lane. Take the second signposted path on the right, crossing the field diagonally to the B6261. Turn right onto the road taking the first footpath to the right signed *Street Lane*. Aim for a stile in the wall, continue forward following the wall, cross a field and

two stiles to join Street Lane. Turn right on the lane and take the footpath on the left signed *Orton*. Continue by the wall and pass through a small gate into a narrow walled lane. Cross the road and footbridge and return to the start on a tarmac path.

Walk 23: Ash Fell Edge

DESCRIPTION: A 4 mile circular walk starting on Access Land and then onto a public footpath before returning to Lytheside Farm and a short road walk passing historic Tarn House built in 1664. **TIME**: 1½ - 2 hours. **START**: Lay-by below cattle grid on the A683 Kirkby Stephen to Sedbergh road, grid NY757037. Walk 30 also skirts Ash Fell and starts from Ravenstonedale.

From the layby walk uphill on the wall side taking in the fine views of the Howgills and Wild Boar Fell. Pass the cairn and continue by the wall side to pass a gate and footpath entering from the right. Approaching the A685 descend left through an old quarry to join a public footpath which skirts around the fell wall. Notice the old walled well above. Continue on the fell wall to pass through Lytheside Farm and join the minor road which leads back to the A683. Turn left on the A683, pass Tarn House and return to the starting point.

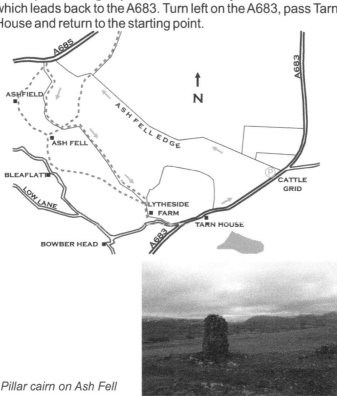

Pillar cairn on Ash Fell

DESCRIPTION: A 4 mile circular walk to Great Ewe Fell on public bridleways although the open ground to the summit is Access Land. **TIME**: 1½ - 2 hours . **START**: Newbiggin-on-Lune just off the A685 Kirkby Stephen to Tebay road.

From the Village Hall on the main street walk towards the A685 and the Garden Centre. Cross the main road and take the right hand fork on a tarmac road which leads to Friar's Bottom Farm. Turn left into a narrow walled public bridleway signed for Ravenstonedale Moor, cross the dismantled railway and bear left to Brownber. At the junction turn right and take the bridleway signed for Bents. Climb on the track to Bents, pass in front of the farmhouse and turn left to continue on the bridleway and pass the Camping Barn. There are some curious sandstone outcroppings here. Pass through the gate and uphill to meet the Coast to Coast path. From here leave the bridleway and traverse north west on open ground to the small summit cairn on Great Ewe Fell. Descend south to pass an obvious cairn of stones and forward to rejoin the fell wall at NY701066. Pass through the gate on the right and forward to a waymark post where turn left to a gate to follow the bridleway down through the next field.

Take the gate at the bottom and continue forward between house and wooden buildings on an obvious fenced access route which continues down to Brownber and the A685.

Walk 25: Oddendale & Hardendale

DESCRIPTION: A 6 mile circular walk on rights of way returning briefly on the Coast-to-Coast route. **TIME**: 2½ - 3 hours. **START**: Shap Village Hall at NY566152.

Walk into Shap Memorial Park and turn left at the top of the field to follow the footpath out. Turn right and right again to join the metalled road and continue over the railway bridge bearing right through buildings. At the field top turn left through a gate into a narrow walled lane. Keep forward through stiles and turn left at the fingerpost signed for Hardendale. Cross the field diagonally, join a wall on the right and cross the motorway footbridge. Turn right and immediately left through a kissing gate continuing forward through two more wall stiles and keeping left of the wall as Hardendale is approached. Join the access lane turn right and immediately left signed for Crosby Ravensworth and Castlehouse Scar. Clear Hardendale and keep forward through three fields to cross the minor road and enter enclosed woodland signed for Haberwain Lane. Exit the woodland by a double stile and make a gradual ascent aiming for a gated fence and forward again to reach Iron Hill. Turn right onto the bridleway and forward through another gate to continue on an obvious green bridleway. Descend to the minor road at Oddendale and after ¼ mile turn right onto the quarry track (Coast to Coast) which follow bearing right to join a footpath which traverses above a field enclosure. As the enclosure recedes descend to a large boulder and bear right to follow the path out to a minor road. Cross the road and continue forward uphill through a gate traversing across The Nab alongside the motorway. Cross the footbridge and bear right across fields to join a junction with a walled lane. Keep right here on the top path signed for Hardendale and Shap.

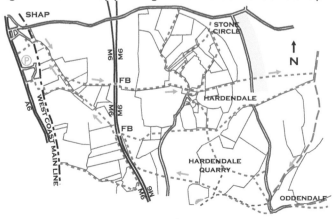

Walk 26: Great & Little Kinmond

DESCRIPTION: A 4½ mile circular walk from Sunbiggin Tarn onto the limestone outcrops. An expansive landscape easily traversed. Return through pasture to Sunbiggin across the heather of Tarn Moor. **TIME**: 1¾ - 2 hours. **START**: Lay-by at cattle grid adjacent to the tarn.

Take the track leading onto Tarn Moor directly from the lay-by and when it joins the main bridleway turn right and follow it north to the gate below Great Kinmond. Enter the enclosure and follow the bridleway uphill to pass through the fence. There is a choice here either to continue on the track by the wall or to branch right across open ground to ascend to a small cairn on the edge of Great Kinmond. Both routes converge again on leaving the enclosure. From the cairn continue north through the limestone outcroppings and aim for the gate in the top left hand corner. Pass through the gate and bear left to follow the wall round (avoiding the need to follow the bridleway slightly further north). Cross the ladder stile over the fence by the wall and immediately left through a small gate giving access onto Little Kinmond. This track returns to Sunbiggin descending gently through a series of field gates as the path proceeds diagonally across pasture. At Sunbiggin Farm the route continues round the perimeter of the farm on an obvious enclosed track finally joining the minor road. Turn left on the road for about ¾ mile and then forward on the bridleway signed for Sunbiggin Tarn. Enter Tarn Moor through a gate and shortly after turn right at a crossroad of tracks to return to Sunbiggin Tarn.

Enter Tarn Moor through a gate and shortly after turn right at a crossroad of tracks to return to Sunbiggin Tarn.

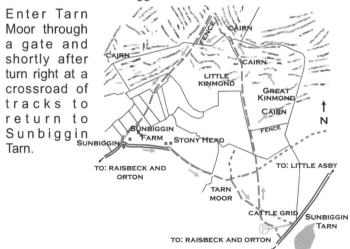

Section 3
Ravenstonedale & Northern Howgills

Location Map for Walks 27 - 40 overleaf
Walk 27: Green Bell
Walk 28: Smardale Bridge, Brownber & Newbiggin
Walk 29: Crosby Garrett circular
Walk 30: Ash Fell
Walk 31: Smardalegill Viaduct
Walk 32: Paradise
Walk 33: Harter Fell & Wandale
Walk 34: Uldale waterfalls
Walk 35: Randygill Top & Kensgriff
Walk 36: Cautley Spout & The Calf
Walk 37: Blease Fell
Walk 38: Uldale Head & Fell Head
Walk 39: Baugh Fell
Walk 40: Black Force, The Spout & Linghaw

Looking south from Green Bell, Howgills

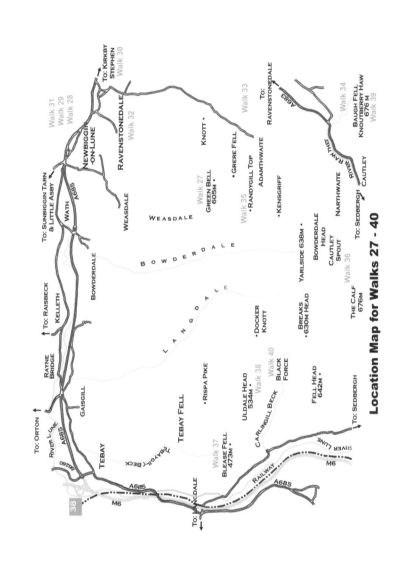

Location Map for Walks 27 - 40

DESCRIPTION: A 6½ mile circular on open fell ascending to 605m (1985ft) with easy going mostly on rough moorland paths. **TIME:** 3 - 4 hours **START:** St Oswalds Church, Ravenstonedale grid NY722042.

Start through the churchyard and left on the road for a ¼ mile. Take the road on left signed for Greenside and after 50 yards take the footpath on the right for Will Hill. Continue next to the wall for about ½ mile finally crossing a field to a small gate. Descend past a barn to a farm gate, bearing right to join the road at Will Hill. Turn left and continue for about ½ mile to a T-junction and take the path left onto the fell signed for Green Bell. There is a path, indistinct in places, and a long steady climb. Keep Pinksey Gill on the right and aim to ascend to the broad flank of Stwarth where the path finally becomes more obvious as it continues to Green Bell. To return bear east on a path which descends to Knoutberry and continue over to join a distinct rutted track on the west flank of Knott and above Wye Garth Gill. Descend keeping the enclosure of Thornthwaite on the left and join an old access track on its northern end which feeds into Wye Garth (fell access point). An obvious path continues down to Kilnmire. Continue on the road and cross the footbridge for access to the village green. Keep to the left to return on the back lane.

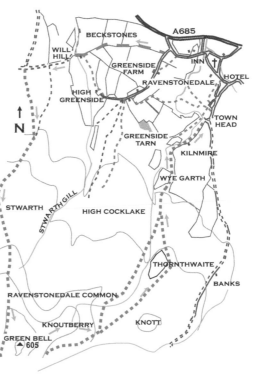

Walk 28: Smardale Br., Brownber & Newbiggin

DESCRIPTION: A 4½ mile circular to an ancient packhorse bridge through enclosed pasture.**TIME:** 2 - 3 hours. **START:** St Oswalds Church, Ravenstonedale grid NY722042.

Walk out of the village on the road, turn right passing the cottages and take the footpath left signed for Smardale. Cross the main road and follow the track on the wall side. The route is waymarked, passes through a gate and as the wall turns away right keep straight forward to cross yet another wall stile. Continue forward above the river and follow the track to Smardale Bridge. Cross the bridge and follow the bridleway through a waymarked gate and continue to Friars Bottom. At the buildings turn left onto the road and immediately right to take the path signed for Ravenstonedale Moor on a narrow walled track. Turn left onto the disused railway and left at the second footpath for Newbiggin. Cross down the field side to the main road. Turn right on the verge and first left onto Newbiggin main street. Walk through the village and after the last building take the sign for Will Hill. Continue down the field edge and pass over an old stile onto a track by the beck and on to Beckstones. By the farm entrance cross the bridge and down the road taking the sign left for High and Low Greenside and immediately left through a blue gate. Cross a footbridge and to the right of a barn continue on the waymarked route through fields to the minor road. Turn left and right at the T-junction to return.

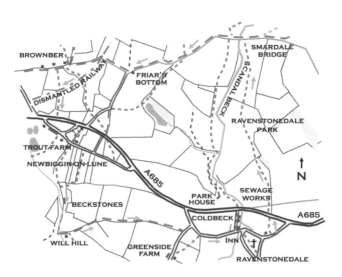

Walk 29: Crosby Garrett Circular

DESCRIPTION: An 8 mile circular crossing Smardale Fell and on to Crosby Garrett returning via ancient Smardale Bridge. **TIME:** 4 - 5 hours. **START:** St Oswalds Church, Ravenstonedale grid NY722042.

Walk into the village and left over the bridge by the hotel. Continue uphill on the road and take the left fork into a narrow lane. Take the footpath signed for Ash Fell and cross the field diagonally to above a small wood and descend to the stream and then forward and uphill to another stile. Continue uphill bearing right to the wallside to take the permissive route signed on the right to traverse round Ashfield farm (waymarked).

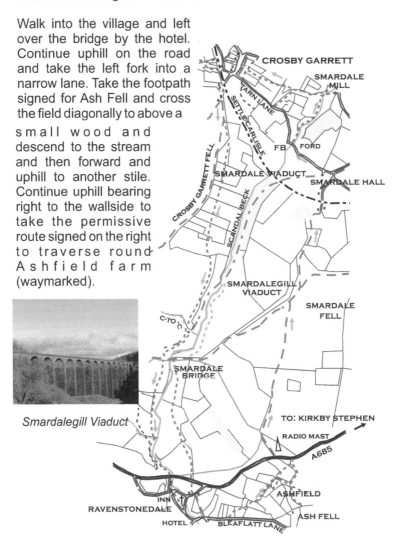

Smardalegill Viaduct

Walk 29: Crosby Garrett Circular

Continue uphill to a stile and cross a lane to another stile. Go straight uphill to Stone House. Take the stile behind Stone House to join a bridleway and turn left to the main road. Turn left down the road and take the bridleway on the right signed for Smardale Fell. Follow the wall side uphill to a gate. Follow this bridleway and after about ½ mile pass through a gate onto Smardale Fell. Continue for another ½ mile to a finger post and continue straight forward (with a wall on the left) for Smardale Hall. Descend to a gate and continue downhil through another gate to where the track swings right above a wood to join a minor road. Cross under the Settle-Carlisle railway and pass Smardale Hall to a T-junction. Turn left and pass the old Station House, bear left and then straight forward - continue down a narrow lane to a ford/ footbridge. Cross and take the footpath on the right signed for Smardale Mill crossing three fields on the riverside to the next footbridge. Turn left here away from the river to follow an old track and after about ¼ mile turn right through a waymarked gate and continue through fields. Pass through another waymarked gate into the remains of a lane and then pass through another gate just to the left. Again continue forward through two fields to a gate which gives access into a green lane for the village. Follow the lane out to the road and turn left and continue straight forward through Crosby Garrett passing under the massive railway viaduct and onto the bridleway signed for Bents. Keep to the left hand track close to the wall and take the waymarked gate on the left. Continue through fields/stiles on a gentle diagonal to the left. Take a stile to arrive above the railway cottages and turn left downhill to pass them. Cross over the bridge and turn right to descend on the path to Smardale Bridge. Join the bridleway at the bridge and turn right and follow the footpath over the stile signed for Ravenstonedale. Continue forward aiming for the lower edge of trees crossing the stile and then keeping to the side of the fence. After the next stile bear slightly right to a yellow post and zig-zag down the slope. Cross the footbridge and join the farm track ahead and leave it on the left as the track climbs uphill continuing by the fence. Pass through a gate and follow the waymarked signs turning right next to a footbridge and go forward under the road bridge to return.

DESCRIPTION: An easy 3 mile walk through fields and a brief section on the lower slopes of Ash Fell. **TIME**: 2 hours. **START:** St Oswalds Church, Ravenstonedale. Walk 23 also visits Ash Fell Edge.

Walk into the village and, at the Black Swan, left over the bridge and immediately right to follow the footpath signed for Low Lane. Keep on the beckside, join the road and turn right to take the footpath on the right signed for Stouphill Gate and Bowber Head. Cross the footbridge and stile and continue on the side of Scandal Beck on a waymarked route. Leave the river bank as you approach a barn ahead and continue diagonally left across the field towards a wood and cross the stile and footbridge. Turn right to continue by a beck towards the barn, ignore the stile and bear left to pass through a waymarked gate and into a lane. Follow this green lane with a stream on the right as it bears round and climbs up to Bowber Head. Turn right and continue out to the road and turn left for ½ mile. Keep right on Bleaflatt Lane, pass Bleaflatt and take the signed footpath on the right. Follow the wall on the left as it turns uphill and continue over a waymarked stile. Walk across the field towards Ash Fell and cross the stile turning left to a gate for access to Ash Fell. Turn right and continue on a walled track signed for Ash Fell road. After a few hundred yards go through a gate onto the fell and turn left (waymarked) to follow the intake wall. Take the gate on the left where a track descends towards Ashfield. Immediately above Ashfield a stile gives permissive access around the perimeter of the farm and outbuildings. Bear right at the waymark post and cross the stile turning left downhill. Cross a waymarked gated stile and continue uphill towards the left corner of a wood. Cross the stile and walk uphill bearing slightly left to re-join Bleaflatt Lane to return.

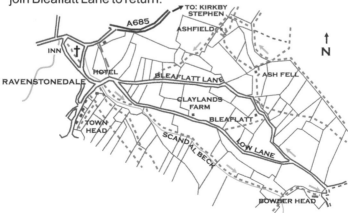

Walk 31: Smardalegill Viaduct

DESCRIPTION: A 4½ mile circular walk to ancient Smardale Bridge and the dismantled Stainmore railway with an extension to Smardale Gill Nature Reserve. **TIME**: 2 - 3 hours. **START:** St Oswalds Church, Ravenstonedale.

Follow the outward route for Walk 28 to Smardale Bridge. Do not cross the bridge but take the bridleway to the right and after a short distance turn left over a stile onto a permissive path which traverses above Scandal Beck.

The path continues for about ½ mile to Smardalegill Viaduct which towers over this narrow valley. At the stile join the disused railway line. Turn right to explore the Nature Reserve perhaps as far as Smardale Viaduct, still carrying the Settle-Carlisle railway. Return by crossing Smardalegill Viaduct to the left and walking down the line. Pass the railway cottages and under a bridge turning left shortly after to join the Coast-to-Coast route down to Smardale Bridge. Join the bridleway at the bridge and turn right to follow the footpath over the stile signed for Ravenstonedale. The return is the same as Walk 29.

Smardalegill Viaduct

DESCRIPTION: A 3 mile stroll to Paradise. **TIME**: 2 hours.
START: St Oswalds Church, Ravenstonedale.

Walk into the village bear right at the Black Swan and up the street for about 200 yards taking the footpath left signed for Lockholme Head. Continue forward on a clear waymarked route through fields with stiles. Keep forward to join Townhead Lane which cross continuing on the signed route for Lockholme Head keeping the beck on your right. Join the bridleway and turn right to pass between the buildings at Row Foot. Continue forward to a gate and through a tree-lined enclosure to another gate to enter Paradise. Follow the wall to the right towards The Green and bear left to continue on the bridleway which traverses back above the tarn. Approach Lockholme through gates and pass through the farmyard to take the access road to Townhead Lane. Turn right, passing Stouphill Gate and left on the signed footpath for Bowber Head. Approach the barn taking the stile to the left continuing forward to cross the field to a gate in the right hand corner. Descend to cross two footbridges over Scandal Beck. Pass the stone barn to take the stile and continue forward taking the footbridge on the left, turn right and continue forward down the field to the gate in the left corner. Keep the beck on the left and continue through fields to a final stile to turn right over a footbridge to Low Lane. Turn left and left again on the signed footpath for Ravenstonedale.

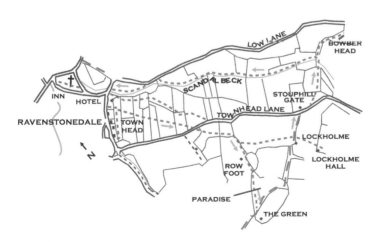

DESCRIPTION: A 7½ mile circular walk starting ancient woodland continuing to open fell and returning on bridleway to Narthwaite. **TIME:** 3 - 4 hours. **START:** Lay-by on the A683 at Rawthey Bridge, grid SD713979.

Cross Rawthey Bridge and take the public footpath over the stile immediately to the left. Cross the footbridge and continue down the bank of the river Rawthey. Take the stile into woodland and exit into a field crossing it to return into Murthwaite Park at a stile. Continue forward briefly but do not cross the stream, turning sharp right onto a bridleway which continues through the woods and out onto open, boggy ground. Pass a barn on the right and through a gate at Murthwaite. Continue straight forward through a smaller black gate and join the farm access road. Follow this out and continue down the bridleway which forks off left signed for Stonely Gill. At the ford bear right to commence the ascent of Harter Fell. From the summit bear north west to Little Harter Fell and then descend to the road serving Adamthwaite. Turn left onto the road. Just before Adamthwaite turn right onto the bridleway signed for Narthwaite. This passes a large modern barn and enters a field enclosure. Continue forward and bear left at a large stone and then exit the enclosure to continue on the bridleway. Note, however, that the track becomes hard to follow as it crosses the lower flank of Wandale Hill. The bridleway reappears as the derelict farm of Mountain View is approached and the route is obvious as it descends steadily thereafter to Narthwaite above the fell wall. Continue through gates into the yard at Narthwaite and bear right to join the access road which continues to descend to the A683. As the track swings right to Handleys Bridge one option is to continue forward into the field to cross the ford encountered in Murthwaite Park at the start of the walk. In wet weather the ford may be difficult to cross and the alternative is to cross Handleys Bridge to join the A683 and return to the lay-by by road.

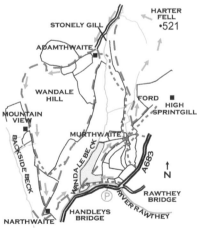

DESCRIPTION: A 5½ or 7 mile circular walk with seclusion, waterfalls, woodland and an extension for the adventurous. **TIME:** 2½ - 3 hours or 4 - 4½ hours. **START:** Lay-by on the A683 at Rawthey Bridge, grid SD713979.

Cross the road below the bridge and use the access gate for the old road across Bluecaster which swings right. Follow to the brow of the hill and take the left fork for Uldale. The bridleway traverses above the river for over a mile to reach a footbridge adjacent to Needle House. The shorter walk returns here to cross this footbridge. Continue on the river bank on an obvious path to Rawthey Gill quarry. After the quarry the way ahead is blocked by another small waterfall which involves an ascent and exposed traverse before returning to the river bank. The next and final waterfall in this section is Uldale Force. The waterfall can be approached on the riverside by an easy scramble but after this the way is impassable. To continue above this gorge return to ascend the steep slope above the waterfall to arrive at a fence and access gate. This is the terminus of the shorter walk. For the return reverse the outward route. Cross at the footbridge to connect with the access road to return on the minor road back to Rawthey Bridge. For the extension note that in wet weather the river bank route through a limestone gorge may be impassable. The alternative is not to pass through the gate but to follow the outside of the fence uphill continuing to ascend and traverse well above the gorge towards Rawthey Gill Foot at the end of the field enclosure on the other side of the gill. To continue into the gorge section pass through the access gate and continue on the river bank to re-join the fence further up. Cross the river and pass through the next access gate to continue into the gorge. A few water crossings will be necessary but the going is easy. Leave the gorge to the right as the stream begins to re-emerge and the way becomes impassable. Continue to follow the river choosing to cross to the left bank when a route becomes obvious and continue to clear the edge of the field enclosure to follow it uphill to an access gate. At this point the Grisedale path is joined and can be followed back to Uldale House. Pass through the yard at the farm and follow the road out to join the minor road.

=WATERFALL
= LIMESTONE GORGE

Walk 35: Randygill Top & Kensgriff

DESCRIPTION: A fairly strenuous 6½ mile circular high level walk with 500m (1650ft) of ascent and some route finding. **TIME:** 2½ - 3 hours. **START:** Roadside just north of Cross Keys Inn, Cautley, grid SD698969.

Cross the footbridge and turn briefly left and then right to join the bridleway to Narthwaite. The route involves a ford crossing at Backside Beck with only some informal stepping stones. Continue uphill on a stony track, pass through a gate and on to Narthwaite. After the first building turn immediately left through another gate and keep right on the waymarked bridleway. At the next gate keep left and continue on the wall side finally joining open fell. The bridleway now continues on a delightful high level path passing the derelict Mountain View farm. After the farm the bridleway becomes less distinct but continue towards Adamthwaite Sike. Bear left as the field enclosure is approached and aim to cross Spen Gill above an obvious ravine. The next objective is Randygill Top and whilst there is no defined path keep above Stockless Gill and continue to climb to join the well defined track connecting Green Bell and Randygill Top turning left to gain the summit.

To reach Kensgriff bear roughly east keeping to the ridge. There is no path initially but one appears once the brief ascent begins. After Kensgriff continue forward to descend to the col. At the col bear left on a slender path which continues on a high level route below the screes of Yarlside terminating at the field enclosure of Westerdale. Continue the descent down the flank of Ben End to return to the footbridge.

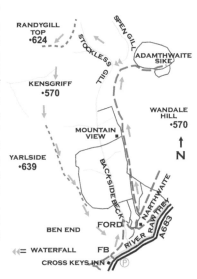

Walk 36: Cautley Spout & The Calf

DESCRIPTION: A popular 4½ mile circular route ascending adjacent to Cautley Spout and Red Gill to The Calf - the highest Howgill summit at 676m (2219ft). Total ascent 1600 feet.   **TIME:** 2½ - 3 hours. **START:** Roadside north of the Cross Keys Inn, Cautley, grid SD698969.

Take the footpath over the footbridge signed for Cautley Spout and follow the gravelled path on the side of the river Rawthey. Continue on this track as it swings right on the bank of Cautley Holme Beck. Reach the foot of the Cautley Spout waterfalls and start the steep ascent which soon becomes stepped. At the head of the waterfall turn left onto a track which crosses Swere Gill. Join Red Gill Beck and continue to follow the beck on an obvious path on the right bank.

Pass Red Gill washfold continuing to ascend to the watershed. Turn right onto a substantial bridleway which leads to The Calf. For the return keep forward on the same track heading north to pass a small tarn on the left.

The track is bound for Bowderdale and starts to descend slowly. A green track branches off to the right to follow Swere Gill on its left bank and Cautley Holme Beck should, in clear weather, be visible far below. This route returns to the outward route at the head of the Cautley Spout waterfall. One option is to descend the steps but an alternative is to traverse left on the track towards Bowderdale Head for a few hundred yards and, after crossing a small stream, take another grassy track that drops back down to the foot of Cautley Spout.

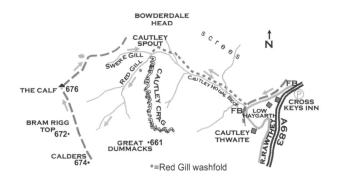

*=Red Gill washfold

DESCRIPTION: A 6 mile circuit of Tebay Gill mostly on footpaths and including lonely Blease Fell. **TIME:** 2½ - 3 hours. **START:** Roadside at Tebay on the A685 at grid NY618046

From the top of the village at Mount Pleasant take the minor road for Gaisgill and turn immediately right (opposite the children's playground) on the tarmac road to cross a cattle grid and join open fell. Bear right and then left to join the wall edge and continue on the track to Tebaygill. Once the field enclosure is cleared leave the track bearing right on the ridge to White Combs. Continue to ascend to Blease Fell on an obvious path. There is no marker for the summit of Blease Fell but there is a pile of stones just beyond where the path ceases. There are fine views of Carlingill and down the Lune Gorge. For the return double back across a pathless, boggy section to pick up another path which continues to Hare Shaw and Knott.

Continue to descend to a farm track at the field enclosure Raw Busk. Follow the track for about ¼ mile and turn left on a footpath for Waskew Head and continue down the track to return to Tebay.

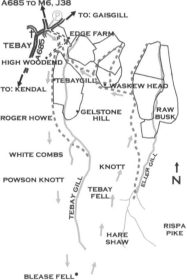

Black Force & Fell Head from Blease Fell

Walk 38: Uldale Head & Fell Head

DESCRIPTION:A strenuous 5 mile circular with 1800 feet of ascent. **TIME**: 4 - 4½ hours. **START**: Carlingill Bridge at grid SD624996. Cross the road bridge and continue up the hill to park on the roadside.

From the bridge take the poor path upstream along the side of Carlingill Beck. If the beck is low it can be forded where the path obviously crosses. Otherwise continue on the right hand bank and take your chances just above where Weasel Gill joins. Behind the sheepfold on the opposite bank an obvious track ascends. Follow this as it zig-zags up the flank of Uldale Head. This route tracks Weasel Gill and is easily followed. Once on the summit edge bear right and continue to the summit. A path then descends east to Blakethwaite Bottom. Continue straight across the smooth grass and forward to ascend to the left of Great Ulgill Beck ensuring enough height is gained to clear the gullies into the beck.
Continue south east to gain height and join an obvious track on the ridge from Docker Knott. This becomes a superb high level traverse as it climbs to Wind Scarth and trends south west to the cairn at Fell Head. At the next cairn (a small pile of stones) take the right fork in the track towards Blake Ridge and then trend due west to continue the descent to the col in front of Linghaw. Cross a track here issuing from the head of Black Force and continue over Linghaw to the final, long descent back to Carlingill.

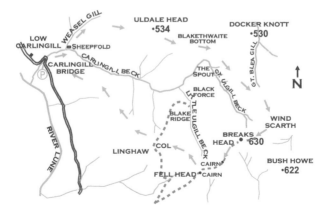

DESCRIPTION: A 10 mile circular walk to a remote location with an isolation normally only found in remote Scotland. On Baugh Fell plateau there is little evidence of paths but on a clear day well worth a visit. **TIME**: Allow at least 5 hours. **START**: Lay-by on A683 at Rawthey Bridge grid SD713979.

For the outward route follow the directions for Walk 34 to Uldale Force and continue to Rawthey Gill Foot. At Rawthey Gill Foot bear right to follow the bed of Rawthey Gill another two miles mainly on its west bank to attain the summit plateau. Ahead is the summit wall and the trig point at Knoutberry Haw.

To return to Rawthey Bridge cross the summit plateau to visit West Baugh Fell Tarn and then bear roughly north west on an easy gradient. A small pile of stones should eventually be encountered on the descent which are a good marker and then bear in front of Bluecaster to reach the bridleway of the outward route.

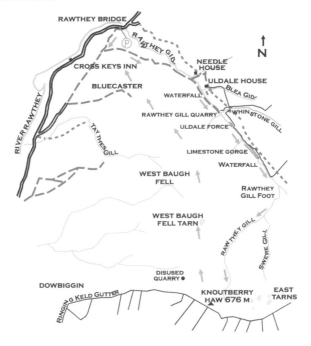

Walk 40: Black Force, The Spout & Linghaw

DESCRIPTION: A 4 mile circular walk in a remote part of the western Howgills with some easy scrambling. Mostly on paths but Carlingill is narrow and stony and in wet weather may be impassable. The return is a satisfying high level traverse and a long descent. **TIME**: 2½ hours. **START**: At Carlingill Bridge grid SD624996. **NOTE:** There are some access restrictions April - June due to nesting birds.

From the bridge at Carlingill follow the south bank of Carlingill Beck. Eventually the route is confined to the bed of the beck because of the steep slopes on either side. Black Force lies to the right but continue forward to reach a 30 foot waterfall at The Spout. Here there is a steep scramble to the left and the way continues on this side of the beck until the grassy flats of Blakethwaite Bottom. The return via Linghaw involves a delightful traverse by doubling back on a faint path on the southern bank of Great Ulgill Beck. The path winds above the Black Force ravine crossing Little Ulgill Beck and continuing below Blake Ridge to an obvious col on the lower slopes of Fell Head. Make the short ascent of Linghaw and then continue on the long descent back to Carlingill Bridge.

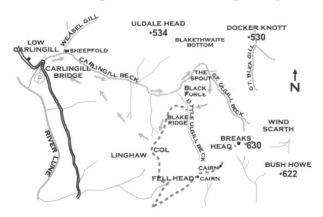

Section 4: The Upper Eden Upland of Hartley Fell, Mallerstang Edge, Wild Boar Fell, The Clouds

Location Map for Walks 41 - 60
Walk 41: Ewbank Scar & Ladthwaite
Walk 42: Great Bell, Mallerstang
Walk 43: Wharton Common
Walk 44: Clouds, Ravenstonedale
Walk 45: Hartley Birkett, Hartley Fell
Walk 46: Lord's Stone & Greyrigg
Walk 47: Tailbridge Hill
Walk 48: Wensleydale Borderland
Walk 49: Dukerdale Circuit
Walk 50: The Nine Standards (from Hartley Fell)
Walk 51: Fells End Quarry & High Pike
Walk 52: Great Bell, Bleakham & High Pike
Walk 53: Elmgill Crag & Raven's Nest
Walk 54: Swarth Fell & Wild Boar Fell from Garsdale (linear)
Walk 55: Wild Boar Fell from Wharton Fell
Walk 56: Mallerstang & Nine Standards Horseshoe
Walk 57: Mallerstang Edge (linear)
Walk 58: Sand Tarn & Wild Boar Fell
Walk 59: The Clouds, Ravenstonedale
Walk 60: The Nine Standards (from Birkdale)

Sand Tarn, Wild Boar Fell

Location Map for Walks 41 - 60

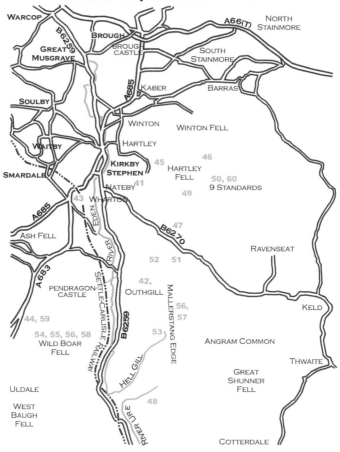

Walk 41: Ewbank Scar & Ladthwaite

DESCRIPTION: A 5 mile circular walk on lower fells and limestone outcrops. **TIME**: 2 - 3 hours. **START**: Kirkby Stephen Market Square.

Proceed east in front of The Cloisters and down Stoneshot leading to Frank's Bridge. Turn right after the bridge and follow the Eden upstream and through the kissing gate. Turn right and continue upstream crossing the footbridge at the end of the field. Continue on the bridleway through woodland and turn left at the first field gate/stile and diagonally uphill to cross the access bridge over the dismantled railway. Continue uphill on the field edge and over two stiles. As the path descends turn left over a stile (barn on right) and immediately left across another stile and descend on a path to approach Ewbank Scar. An obvious path traverses through the woods and climbs parallel to a massive limestone outcrop. At the top of the wood cross a stile and immediately left through a field gate to continue uphill adjacent to Ladthwaite Beck until a stile in the (broken) fence. Continue forward following the beck where the path skirts Birkett Hill. Cross the stile into a field and continue forward towards Ladthwaite crossing the footbridge before the house. Turn left at Ladthwaite on the access track out to the road. Turn left on the road to pass Hartley Quarry. After Merrygill House turn left over a footbridge and into the village turning left into a lane in front of Saltpie Hall to rejoin the outward route.

Walk 42: Great Bell, Mallerstang

DESCRIPTION: A 2 mile circular walk starting approx. 4 miles south of Kirkby Stephen. Remains of lead workings. A steep ascent in the first section. **TIME**: 1 - 1½ hours. **START**: Roadside on the B6259 south of Nateby, grid NY778046.

Cross the stile to access the fell just north of Dalefoot. Bear right uphill to meet the boundary wall and continue on the track above the wall. Soon a track turns off left uphill to an old lead mine. Follow this track as it turns sharp left and then ascend to the right keeping a dry, shallow gully to the right. Cross another track and continue uphill to a rock gully. Bear right and follow a faint path a short way and then bear left up-

-hill again for Great Bell. There are further lead workings in this area. Beyond Great Bell another old miner's track drops away north towards Ridding House. Follow this until it joins a wall at Kitchen Gill. Do not cross the stile but turn left to return on a path which contours above the wall. The wall bears right to the road and a stile giving access for the return.

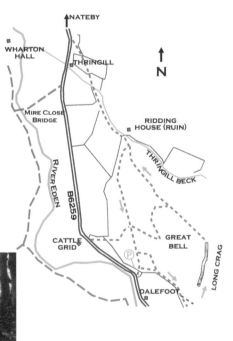

Walk 43: Wharton Common

DESCRIPTION: A level 2 mile circular walk starting approx. 4 miles south of Kirkby Stephen. The walk can be extended by starting from the minor road to Wharton Dykes (first left on the A683). Grid NY759059. **TIME**: 1 hour. **START**: Roadside on the 'Tommy Road', grid NY763039. Take the A683 Sedbergh road and second left for Outhgill.

Head north onto the common and initially stay close to the wall on the left until slightly higher ground is reached. From here bear diagonally right across the common on one of the many paths or tracks. There is a gap between enclosed fields which leads to a bridleway that is adjacent to the railway line. Follow this broad track as it bears right and returns to the 'Tommy road'.

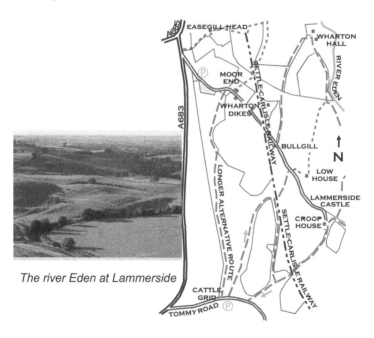

The river Eden at Lammerside

Walk 44: Clouds, Ravenstonedale

DESCRIPTION: A   2 mile circular walk exploring the extensive limestone outcrops below Wild Boar Fell. **TIME**: 1 - 1½ hours. **START**: Roadside approx 9 miles south of Kirkby Stephen adjacent to the A685 at grid NY734008. See also **Walk 59** in this section.

There are many alternative routes through the outcrops. An old track meanders uphill through the limestone passing close to a field wall which leads up to Dale Slack and the ridge. From the ridge continue south or explore below among the boulders. There are extensive surface lead workings. As the ridge peters out there is another old track which returns back to two limekilns by the road. Return by the road or on the lower slopes of Clouds.

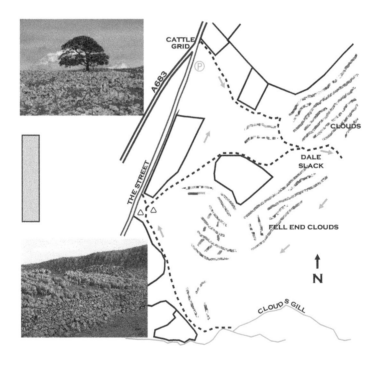

Walk 45: Hartley Birkett, Hartley Fell

DESCRIPTION: A 1½ mile circular walk over Hartley Birkett hill visiting the extensive remains of lead working. **TIME**: up to 2 hours. **START**: Hartley Fell road end at NY799075, a few spaces here or further back down the road. NOTE: Hartley Birkett is not registered common land but was defined as open country under new access rights (CRoW) legislation. Avoid disturbing livestock or attempt to cross walls or fences with no appropriate access.

Continue to the fell gate, do not pass through but bear left up a grassy bank inside the fell wall. Continue uphill and inside the wall as it ascends the summit of Birkett Hill. From here the upper reaches of the lead workings are evident. Descend into the dome where there are various abandoned shafts and dressing floors. Lower down the slope there is the outline of a reservoir and on the flank of the fell beyond the course of an old mill race is visible and another reservoir just east of Birkett Beck. Continue to descend into an area where the hill has been excavated by hushing. To the left onto the western flank of Birkett Hill there are further hushes and old shafts. The workings continue beyond the fell wall west of Birkett Beck. For access follow the inside of the wall towards Fell House and use the fell gate (tucked away at the foot of Little Longrigg Fell) turning right to find workings and hushes amongst the limestone outcrops.

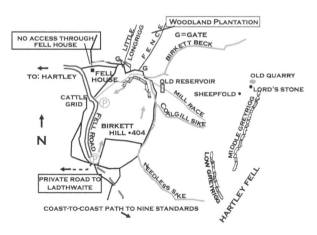

Walk 46: Lord's Stone & Greyrigg

DESCRIPTION: A 4 mile circular walk on open fell. Navigation skills needed in poor visibility although there are landmarks en route. **TIME:** 2 - 2½ hours **START:** Hartley Fell road end at grid NY799075.

Return down the road and bear right just before the bridge. Follow the dry stream bed and cross it to pass some stock pens on the left and keep forward through the gorse and join an obvious track from Fell House to reach the access gate by the fell wall. Alternatively the fenced enclosure can be cleared if preferred using the two lower access gates. Continue to trend uphill and towards Birkett Beck. Cross the beck as the ground levels out traversing right to climb gently to Lord's Stone then continue south on the edge for about 150 yards to a circular sheepfold and ascend east on a faint path to Middle Greyrigg. Then turn right and traverse the edge for 100 yards and again bear left to continue east to High Greyrigg. Pass to the right of Greyrigg sheepfold on an indistinct path. Attain the outcrop of High Greyrigg and again turn right and continue on this edge for ¼ mile before ascending again, this time diagonally, to the grassy level of Low Greenside. There is no path but as you climb you will pass through the Greyrigg Pits coal workings. Continue south down Low Greenside and above the old shafts. The return route is on an old miners track marked on the 1:25000 scale OS map as a bridleway which continues south to join the Coast-to-Coast path. Turn right onto a well made track and continue downhill to return.

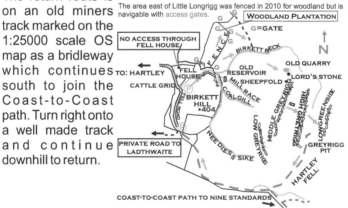

Walk 47: Tailbridge Hill

DESCRIPTION: An easy 1½ mile circular mainly on grass with a gentle ascent to the summit cairn. Superb views across the Eden valley. **TIME:** Approx. 1 hour. **START:** On the unfenced B6270 Nateby - Keld road ¼ mile east of the road summit, grid NY809043.

From the B6270 follow the public bridleway signed for Rollinson Haggs and Hartley. After nearly ¼ mile take the left branch when the track divides. Follow this and then leave the track and aim for the cairn on Tailbridge. As the summit is approached there are the remains of a 'Y' shaped shelter (created from the limestone) to the right. Ascend to the cairn. For a shorter walk there is the option to return down the edge back to the starting point. The alternative is to descend steeply north towards Nateby Cow Close and then contour round the base of the hill and passing a series of old coal excavations incorrectly marked on the 1:25000 OS map as shake holes. Return on the road.

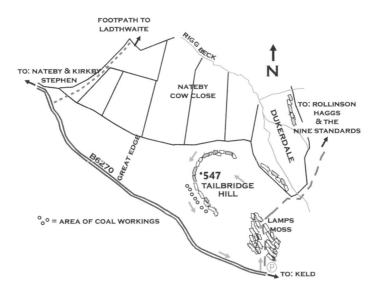

Walk 48: Wensleydale Borderland

DESCRIPTION: A 10 mile circular in a northern corner of the Yorkshire Dales. **TIME:** 3 - 4 hours. **START:** At Aisgill Cottages on the B6259 on the Cumbria-North Yorkshire boundary, grid SD778963.

From Aisgill Cottages take the unmade road signed for Hellgill and cross the bridge over the Settle-Carlisle railway. The road forks just before it meets the river Eden and turns sharply right to continue up to Hellgill to join the Highway.

Cross Hell Gill bridge and take the left fork after 220 metres. The Highway contours along the fell side south passing High Hall and continues to contour above the enclosure wall at around 1300 feet. Pass another wooded gorge, through a gate and pass an old lime kiln as the route twists and clings to the hill side. Another ruin, High Way, is just visible below. After a substantial wooden gate a building is reached -High Dyke- a ruinous 16th century droving inn with associated buildings and enclosures.

At this point the route leaves the Highway and descends to Lunds Church. Turn right through the gates of High Dyke. The route now cuts diagonally right down the hill side and care is needed as the path is indistinct although the white walls of Lunds Church will soon be visible. Keep the wall enclosing the field around High Dyke on your right and descend crossing a branch wall as it turns downhill. Continue to descend to the stile in the next wall running vertically downhill. Continue at roughly 45°aiming for a wall corner above a roofed barn and a large sycamore tree.

From here to Shaws the path contours the fell side. At the roofed barn turn right to cross a small footbridge and forward to cross an iron gate. Pass below a derelict barn and through a stile and forward again to cross a gated fence just above a barn. Follow the broken wall on the left to the footpath sign at Shaws and turn left down the slope for Lunds, through a wall gate and over the wooden footbridge. Bear slightly left to pass through a stile into the farmyard. Continue straight forward crossing a stile into the field and over the footbridge to reach Lunds Church.

Walk 48: Wensleydale Borderland

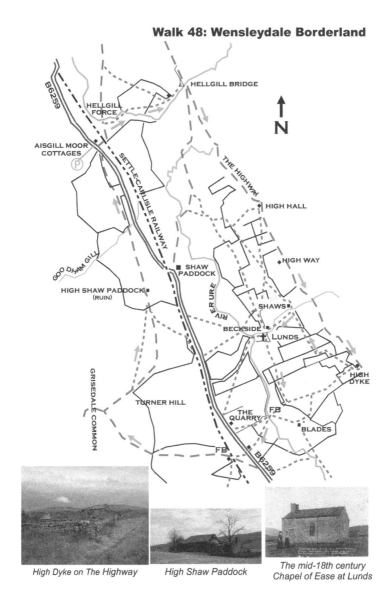

N

B6259

HELLGILL BRIDGE

HELLGILL FORCE

AISGILL MOOR COTTAGES

P

SETTLE-CARLISLE RAILWAY

THE HIGHWAY

HIGH HALL

GOODHAM GILL

HIGH WAY

SHAW PADDOCK

HIGH SHAW PADDOCK (RUIN)

RIVER URE

SHAWS

BECKSIDE

LUNDS

HIGH DYKE

GRISEDALE COMMON

TURNER HILL

THE QUARRY

FB

BLADES

FB

B6259

High Dyke on The Highway   *High Shaw Paddock*   The mid-18th century
Chapel of Ease at Lunds

Walk 48: Wensleydale Borderland

Cross the graveyard and pass through the stile to ascend Cowshaw Hill. From the signpost descend on a small path to the wall and stile below and then aim for the next stile by the white gate at the bottom of the hill. Cross and follow the wall on its left side until a stile is reached by a fence and turn right to reach Blades footbridge over the river Ure. Take the left gate just after crossing the bridge and continue up the field to the stile by a barn. The path then reaches the B6259 just to the left of the farmhouse. Cross the road and take the path signed for *East Mudd Becks* to the iron footbridge over the Settle to Carlisle railway line. Cross the line and turn right in front of the cottages to the stile by the iron gate. Ascend the hillside - little remains of what might have been an ancient track but aim for the trees and wall on the skyline ahead. Maintain contact with the wall on the right and ascend to the ladder stile at the top of the hill to reach Grisedale Common.

After crossing the stile turn right to follow the wall over Turner Hill. When the wall turns right follow it through the gate. Present day maps indicate a bridleway through to High Shaw Paddock which would also have been an ancient track linking this area with Mallerstang and Kirkby Stephen. However until just before High Shaw Paddock not much of this track remains although it is possible to pick up its line after the first part of this section.

A recommended line is to aim for the source of a stream that emerges from the limestone. A very small path branches away from the wall after a few hundred yards and this can be followed. The head of the stream can be crossed easily and the old track should begin to be visible after descending a little more. The outline of High Shaw Paddock, once in view, should also assist with route finding as this ruinous farm is the next place to be visited. Enter the paddock of High Shaw ruin by the gate and pass in front of the building leaving by another gate. The old bridleway now continues above the wall to Aisgill. Ahead the familiar outline of Wild Boar Fell provides a fitting back drop for the conclusion of the walk

Walk 49: Dukerdale Circuit

DESCRIPTION: A 6 mile circular starting at Hartley Fell road end with a round of remote Dukerdale on rough moorland returning via Ladthwaite. **TIME:** 3 - 4 hours. **START:** Grid NY799075.

Join the bridleway keeping right at the sign for the Coast to Coast and Nine Standards continuing by the wall. After about ¼ mile the path bears left and uphill and continues to climb away from the fell wall. The ground above the wall can be wet so the route outlines a continued ascent to the ruin at Rollinson on an old track (marked as a bridleway). There are two waymark posts on this section. Turn right at Rollinson and descend on the bridleway and eventually rejoin the wall. Follow the wall as it trends right and descends to Duker Beck. Cross the beck, keep to the wall and as the wall trends right above Dukerdale continue straight forward on an obvious track which, after about ½ mile, climbs towards Tailbridge Hill. At the T-junction turn right to descend to the wall enclosing Nateby Cow Close and continue for just over one mile until adjacent to the quarry at grid NY789062. Cross into Nateby Cow Close at the gate and follow the footpath across the field crossing the stile and continuing by the wall. Descend to the trees, cross a stile and between trees. Cross the bridge at the rear of Ladthwaite turning left to join the private access road. Turn right and follow the road out to the start point on Hartley Fell road.

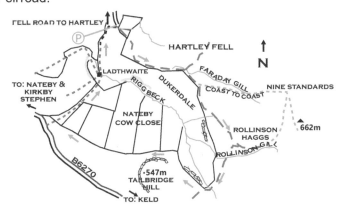

Walk 50: The Nine Standards

DESCRIPTION: A 5 mile circular walk to the local landmark of pillar cairns. **TIME:** 2 - 2½ hours. **START:** Hartley Fell road end grid NY799075 where there are a few spaces otherwise further back down the road.

Follow the bridleway onto Hartley Fell and continue uphill adjacent to the wall. After nearly a mile pass the signpost for Nine Standards (do not take) and continue adjacent to the wall on an obvious track. After ¼ mile the track swings left away from the wall and continues to ascend. At the same time it enters wet ground where the track is obscured. Continue uphill bearing slightly right. The route here has two waymarked posts and eventually the track becomes more obvious again as the cairn at Rollinson Haggs comes into view. This track joins a Coast-to-Coast alternative route just above the cairn. Turn left and follow an obvious path which ascends north to the viewpoint just south of Nine Standards. Proceed forward to Nine Standards. For the return descent bear left (west) on a well made path which joins Faraday Gill and then the outward route.

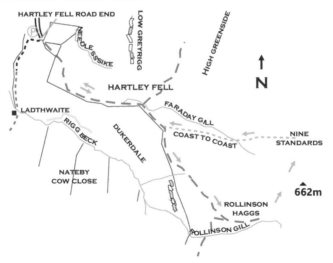

Walk 51: Fells End Quarry & High Pike

DESCRIPTION: A 2 mile circular walk with some route finding using an old quarry track. Superb views across the Eden valley. See also Walk 52. **TIME:** 2 hours. **START:** On the unfenced B6270 Nateby - Keld road grid NY809043.

From the B6270 head south downhill. There is a track which continues up Careless Bank. At about 550 metres leave Careless Bank and traverse west (there is no path) to pass well beneath the crags above. An old quarry track can be picked up from here. Continue along the track as it skirts the crags and swings south and eventually climbs up to the quarry site and a large walled enclosure. Continue south down the quarry edge to the prominent pillar cairn. There is a faint path which continues straight uphill and from where the cairn on High Pike can be reached. To return continue on the path north to descend Careless Bank to reach the B6270.

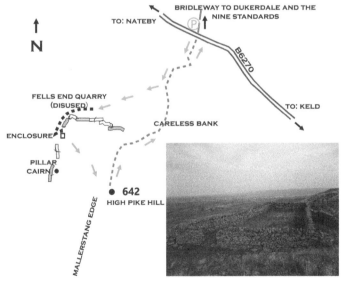

Enclosure at Fells End Quarry (disused).

Walk 52: Great Bell, Bleakham, High Pike & Fells End Quarry

DESCRIPTION: A 7½ mile circular rough moorland walk including the rarely visited areas of Bleakham and High Brae. A marked absence of defined paths. **TIME:** 3½ - 5 hours. **START:** B6259 south of Nateby, grid NY782043.

Park on the roadside, cross the stile and head uphill. Summer bracken makes a traverse through (and beyond) the lead workings above Dalefoot difficult. An alternative is to approach Long Crag directly where there is a convenient lead hush (marked as a stream on modern OS maps) which runs diagonally up the hillside.

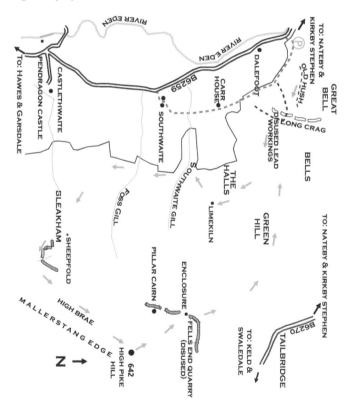

Walk 52: Great Bell, Bleakham, High Pike & Fells End Quarry

Ascend the crag and continue south - there is no path but aim to clear the highest field enclosures to reach an area called The Halls. In clear weather an isolated limekiln should become visible just north of Southwaite Gill at about 420 metres. Bleakham Scar is the next objective after the limekiln and a direct route is pathless over wet and boggy ground.

An alternative is to descend back to the fell wall towards Southwaite Gill. There is a minor path here which traverses the deep cuttings of Southwaite and Foss Gills and continues on to Gale Sike. After Foss Gill head diagonally uphill towards Bleakham Scar. Ascend the steep shoulder of Bleakham Scar to reach an area called High Brae. There are some distinctive excavations above High Brae which are little documented. From Bleakham continue to ascend eastward. After gaining the slightly higher ground towards the Edge an old track traverses north-south on the hillside. The track is indistinct but recognisable in clear conditions. Follow this for about 100 metres. Below the track is an abandoned drinking trough. The slopes above consist of large spoil heaps, most likely for coal. The workings consist of two separate sections on the slope above and continue north for about 200 metres. The second section is not obvious from below but by ascending the slope a short distance the extent of the workings become evident. To continue to High Pike follow the second excavation and aim for an obvious rock outcrop. It is a short distance from here to the summit cairn of High Pike. To reach Fells End Quarry there is a small path from High Pike to the quarry which runs diagonally across the fell side in a northwest direction and concludes at the large stone enclosure perched on the fell edge. To return to the start of the walk descend to the next level at the base of the quarry. There is a minor path which continues west across to Green Hill and Long Crag although it can be difficult to follow consistently but in any event the going is easy and downhill.

Walk 53: Elmgill Crag & Raven's Nest

DESCRIPTION: A 5 mile circular starting on 'The Highway' and continuing on a pathless route to the great boulder field of Elmgill Crag. After Raven's Nest the route returns on The Highway. **TIME:** 2 - 2½ hours. **START:** Car park at Boggle Green on the B6259 at grid NY783005.

Below the car park take the old road signed *Public Way* and continue on this until adjacent to an electric pylon on the left. Bear left towards the limekiln and quarry continuing uphill behind the limekiln and between a stream to the left and a dry gully in an area called 'Knowes'. Continue uphill to a ruinous pinfold. From here traverse right for about 200 metres and then climb straight uphill on an obvious raised grassy mound on a faint path. On reaching the boulder field traverse right across reeds towards the higher ground of Elmgill and continue to gain height to reach a well preserved sheepfold. Continue to traverse and climb diagonally right across the boulder field and clearing reedy ground. Continue at the same height as reed gives way to grass. The outline of Raven's Nest will be visible above as the end of Mallerstang Edge is approached. Skirt the base of Raven's Nest to gain

access. Continue to ascend south to gain the start of the Edge at a cairn where the track climbs gently up from Hell Gill Bridge. To return continue south briefly down the Hell Gill track and then bear west on a pathless descent to re-join The Highway. The sculpture 'Water Cut' will become visible which stands close to the track just north of Hanging Lund Scar. Join the track and turn right to return.

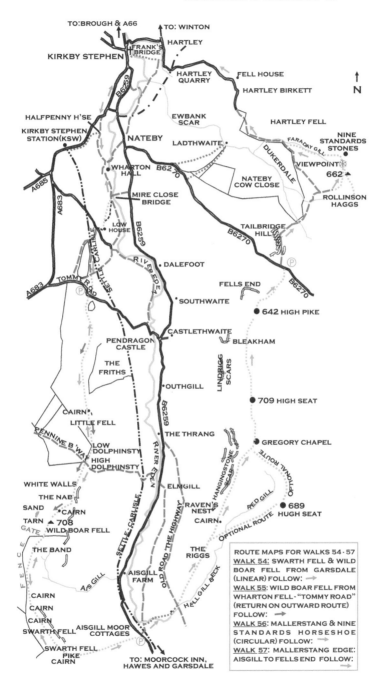

TO: BROUGH & A66
TO: WINTON
HARTLEY
FRANK'S BRIDGE
KIRKBY STEPHEN
HARTLEY QUARRY
FELL HOUSE
HARTLEY BIRKETT
N
HALFPENNY H'SE
EWBANK SCAR
HARTLEY FELL
KIRKBY STEPHEN STATION (KSW)
NATEBY
LADTHWAITE
FARADAY GILL
NINE STANDARDS STONES
DUKERDALE
VIEWPOINT
662
WHARTON HALL
B6270
NATEBY COW CLOSE
ROLLINSON HAGGS
A685
A683
MIRE CLOSE BRIDGE
LOW HOUSE
B6259
TAILBRIDGE HILL
B6270
SETTLE - CARLISLE
River Eden
DALEFOOT
FELLS END
B6270
A683
TOMMY ROAD
SOUTHWAITE
● 642 HIGH PIKE
CASTLETHWAITE
BLEAKHAM
PENDRAGON CASTLE
LINDRIGG SCARS
THE FRITHS
OUTHGILL
● 709 HIGH SEAT
B6259
CAIRN
LITTLE FELL
THE THRANG
● GREGORY CHAPEL
PENNINE B'WAY
LOW DOLPHINSTY
River Eden
HIGH DOLPHINSTY
HANGINGSTONE SCAR
OPTIONAL ROUTE
WHITE WALLS
ELMGILL
THE NAB
SAND
CAIRN
TARN ▲ 708
WILD BOAR FELL
RAVEN'S NEST
CAIRN
RED GILL
● 689 HUGH SEAT
SETTLE-CARLISLE
OPTIONAL ROUTE
GATE
THE BAND
OLD ROAD THE HIGHWAY
THE RIGGS
FENCE
As Gill
HELL GILL BECK
CAIRN
CAIRN
CAIRN
SWARTH FELL
AISGILL FARM
AISGILL MOOR COTTAGES
SWARTH FELL PIKE CAIRN
TO: MOORCOCK INN, HAWES AND GARSDALE

ROUTE MAPS FOR WALKS 54 - 57

WALK 54: SWARTH FELL & WILD BOAR FELL FROM GARSDALE (LINEAR) FOLLOW: →

WALK 55: WILD BOAR FELL FROM WHARTON FELL - "TOMMY ROAD" (RETURN ON OUTWARD ROUTE) FOLLOW: →

WALK 56: MALLERSTANG & NINE STANDARDS HORSESHOE (CIRCULAR) FOLLOW: →

WALK 57: MALLERSTANG EDGE: AISGILL TO FELLS END FOLLOW: →

Walk 54: Swarth Fell & Wild Boar Fell from Garsdale

DESCRIPTION: A high level 14 mile linear walk using the Settle-Carlisle rail link to Garsdale from Kirkby Stephen. **TIME: 5 - 6** hours. **START:** Kirkby Stephen (KSW) station grid NY763066. NOTE: There is a public footpath to the station from Kirkby Stephen - see **Walk 9.**

From Garsdale descend to the main road. Take the footpath across the road, pass close to the Clough river and continue through fields to Blakes Mire. Join the minor Grisedale road at Rowantree and turn right to walk up the road to pass East House and reach Grisedale Common. At the Common turn left onto a substantial bridleway and bear right to make a pathless ascent of Grisedale Brow to reach the watershed. Cross the fence and continue left uphill to Swarth Fell Pike. Continue to ascend gently, the fence becomes a substantial wall on the plateau of Swarth Fell. Follow the wall as it bears slightly right and descend to a small tarn. The wall reverts to a fence which the path follows for some distance as it again ascends towards Wild Boar Fell and then the path bears right. The fence can be followed (and may be useful in mist) but the path is obvious. As the summit plateau is reached there is a gate in the fence. Cross and continue north over the summit plateau on an indistinct path to reach the trig point.

For the return to Kirkby Stephen there is a good path. Continue north across the summit plateau to The Nab and descend steeply down the ridge of White Walls to High Dolphinsty. Cross the Pennine Bridleway and follow the wall down to Low Dolphinsty. The path leaves the wall and continues on the ridge over Little Fell. Bear left away from The Friths keeping more or less on the ridge and continue forward onto Greenlaw Rigg to reach the Tommy Road.

There are route choices here. For the Station descend left on the road and as the road climbs bear right on to the common, pass between two limekilns and join the enclosure wall on the left and then aim for NY759059 which gives access to the minor road that joins the A683 and the A685 which passes Kirkby Stephen Station.

For Kirkby Stephen town cross the 'Tommy Road' and continue forward parallel with the railway line (keep left of the line) and cross the line at the access bridge after ½ mile. Continue forward and at the minor road turn left and at Bullgill turn right on the bridleway for Wharton Hall. From Wharton Hall either follow the concrete access road to Halfpenny House (NY769071) or take the bridleway north of the Hall which crosses the river Eden to Nateby and thence to Kirkby Stephen.

Walk 55: Wild Boar Fell from Wharton Fell

DESCRIPTION:A fine 4 mile 'out and back' approach to the summit on the north ridge mostly on good paths. **TIME**: 3 - 4 hours. **START**: On the 'Tommy Road' at grid NY767036. Route map before Walk 54.

From the road proceed south to join the ridge on Greenlaw Rigg. Keep to the right of the 'lonely field' to join an obvious track. The route continues adjacent to The Friths more or less on the ridge. Ascend to Little Fell and continue on the descent to Low Dolphinsty to join an enclosure wall. Climb a short steep section and follow the wall to High Dolphinsty where the Pennine Bridleway crosses between Mallerstang and Ravenstonedale. Continue forward to ascend the final section of White Walls to The Nab. From The Nab the summit cairn is set back on the plateau about ½ mile to the south west and is reached on an obvious path. To complete a circuit of the plateau proceed south east to the cairns at High White Scar from where there are fine views into Mallerstang and south across the Dales. Return on the edge back to The Nab to continue the descent back to 'Tommy Road'.

Looking south to Wild Boar Fell

Walk 56: Mallerstang & Nine Standards Horseshoe

DESCRIPTION: A strenuous 23 mile high level circular walk requiring navigation skills in poor weather. **TIME**: 6 - 9 hours. **START**: There is large public car park adjacent to Kirkby Stephen Grammar School with access from Christian Head. Route map before Walk 54.

From Market Square go south on the main road (A685), over the railway bridge and take the first road left to Wharton Hall. Pass through Wharton Hall and continue south on the farm road to Low House. Follow the farm road out to the minor road and cross the road to join a bridleway over the Settle-Carlisle line. Turn immediately left after the railway bridge and continue adjacent to the railway line to join the Tommy Road. Cross the road and continue straight forward to start the ascent of Wild Boar Fell. **See route description for Walk 55.** From the trig point bear south west (the path is indistinct here) to meet a gate in the fence. Pass through and continue on a path which branches away from the fence and descends above The Band to rejoin the fence for the approach to Swarth Fell.

Continue to ascend Swarth Fell on an obvious track adjacent to a wall and cross the stony plateau to Swarth Fell Pike. From the Pike bear east for a pathless descent to Aisgill. A gate at the foot of the fell gives access to the B6259. Cross the road and take the signed bridleway/farm track that crosses the railway and winds up to Hell Gill Bridge.

Join The High Way and turn left briefly before bearing right off the bridleway aiming for The Riggs keeping to the left of Red Gill. There is a track which leads up to the cairn at SD796987 in front of Raven's Nest and continues onto the edge. The path is fairly obvious although care is needed in poor visibility. Continue on to High Seat and then the long descent onto the plateau which leads to High Pike. The path is less obvious here but emerges once grass is reached towards High Pike. From High Pike the path continues north-east down Careless Bank and joins the B6270 at Tailbridge. Take the signed route for Rollinson Haggs and follow this bridleway through limestone pavement over Lamps Moss to Dukerdale Head. Continue north-east to Rollinson Haggs climbing to the viewpoint on Nine Standards and the field cairns. Descend east on a good path towards Faraday Gill and follow this to Hartley Fell road. Continue on the road, pass Hartley Quarry and as the road levels out take a left turn to cross Hartley Beck over a small stone footbridge. Turn right to pass a terrace of houses and left at Salt Pie Hall onto a tarmac path that leads down to Frank's Bridge in Kirkby Stephen.

Walk 57: Mallerstang Edge; Aisgill to Fells End

DESCRIPTION: A high level 6 mile linear traverse of Gregory Chapel, High Seat and High Pike with an option to include Hugh Seat. Open fell mostly on path but not to Hugh Seat. **TIME**: 2½ - 3 hours. **START**: Start at Aisgill on the B6259 grid SD778963. Limited space adjacent to Aisgill Moor Cottages but roadside places to park close by. Route map before Walk 54.

Take the signed bridleway at the end of Aisgill Cottages, cross the railway bridge and follow the track to Hell Gill Beck. A brief diversion here to the left provides an opportunity to view the graceful waterfall of Hell Gill Force. Continue by turning right up the track that leads to Hell Gill Bridge. On joining The High Way turn left and then immediately bear right towards The Riggs. There is a path which continues onto Mallerstang Edge just above Raven's Nest and then to Gregory Chapel.

HUGH SEAT ROUTE: For a detour to Hugh Seat follow Red Gill after leaving The High Way and continue more or less to its source and then make for Lady's Pillar on Hugh Seat. To reach Gregory's Chapel (a distinctive pillar cairn and shelter) continue north west on an obvious escarpment.

The route over the remainder of the Edge is mostly on a path although this becomes less evident after High Seat but there are sections in the peat which have been eroded by walkers. After the cairn at High Pike there is an obvious path and this leads off Fells End down Careless Bank to join the B6270.

Mallerstang Edge looking north

Walk 58: Wild Boar Fell from Stennerskeugh via Sand Tarn

DESCRIPTION: A 6 mile circular walk on open fell. Route finding required on the final outward section. Return on the Pennine Bridleway. **TIME**: 3 hours. **START**: Roadside at Stennerskeugh on the minor road off the A683 at the start of the Pennine Bridleway grid NY743014.

Take the bridleway signed for Mallerstang. After passing The Green House the walled track is unmade and continues to the open fell. Pass through the gate and bear right on an old, rutted track which roughly follows the fell boundary wall. Ascend to the first obvious limestone outcrops of The Clouds and then bear south-east towards Wild Boar Fell.It is worth not straying too far towards Greenrigg Moss and there is a path of variable quality which passes a ruined sheepfold. Continue to climb east where the path disappears and passes through a boggy section. Once the flank of Wild Boar Fell is in view bear right to gain Sand Tarn. Continue up the steep flank to the summit plateau and the trig point. Cross the plateau north to the cairn on The Nab. For the return descend on an obvious path down to High Dolphinsty by way of White Walls to join the Pennine Bridleway. Pass through a gate to continue down this well made track to the fell access point at the start of the walk.

Walk 59: Clouds, Ravenstonedale

DESCRIPTION: An easy 2 mile circular walk amidst limestone outcrops and old lead workings. **TIME**: 1 - 2 hours. **START**: Roadside just off the A683 Sedbergh road grid NY730448. See also **Walk 44** in this section with a slightly different route.

From the roadside ascend diagonally right to negotiate the lower limestone outcrops to reach a large enclosure and an obvious old track which continues up to Dale Slack. Above Dale Slack bear right on level ground to continue south behind the limestone escarpment. Keep close to the limestone and after about ½ mile descend between two outcrops to the remains of an old reservoir. Lower down there has been extensive hushing. To continue the walk bear west across the limestone and find two distinct cairns which mark an access through the limestone where there are further lead workings. Contour north on an obvious corridor through the limestone and descend to the walled enclosure encountered on the outward journey. Continue to traverse above the enc-

-losure. Notice some caves high above in the limestone which are accessible from a connecting ledge. It is thought that these caves were originally excavated in the search for lead later in the nineteenth century. At the end of the enclosure descend to the old track encountered on the outward journey.

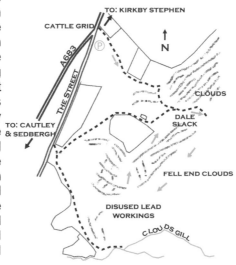

Walk 60: The Nine Standards

DESCRIPTION: A 9 mile fairly strenuous circular fell walk in a remote landscape following Coast-to-Coast alternatives across delicate habitat. Route finding skills an advantage in poor weather. **TIME**: 4½ hours. **START**: Lay-by on the B6270 Nateby-Keld road at Rowantree Gill grid Ny831028. Route map next page.

Walk down the road towards Keld for a hundred yards and turn left onto a shooter's track which climbs onto the fell and descends to a shooting cabin. Cross Ney Gill above the cabin and continue down the Gill along a line of grouse butts. Take the signed route left for the C-to-C route just before Black Sike and then follow the obvious path up Whitsundale Beck. At Craygill Sike trend west and begin a long gentle waymarked ascent to the watershed where a fingerpost indicates route choices. Take note that the return from here is a left turn to White Mossy Hill but to reach Nine Standards turn right. Continue up to the trig point then a viewfinder cairn and finally the Nine Standards. Retrace to the fingerpost at the turning point and continue forward toward White Mossy Hill. There is some peat bog in the vicinity but bearing slightly right around this area should help. At White Mossy Hill the distant prospect of Birkdale Tarn comes into view. Continue along an obvious (but slightly vague) path as it trends down Coldbergh Edge. A pile of stones and a pillar cairn will become more distinct both of which lie on route. Just after the pillar cairn an access track runs off the edge to the right but ignore this and continue forward with some waymark posts in view. Cross a small wooden footbridge and continue the descent to join the shooter's track encountered on the outward route.

cont...

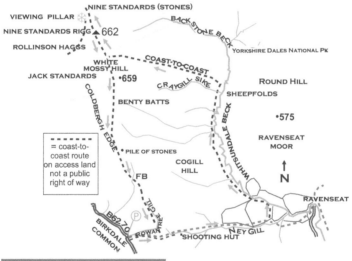

NINE STANDARDS (STONES)

VIEWING PILLAR

NINE STANDARDS RIGG ▲ 662

ROLLINSON HAGGS

BACK STONE BECK

Yorkshire Dales National Pk

WHITE
MOSSY HILL

COAST-TO-COAST

JACK STANDARDS

•659

CRAYGILL SIKE

BENTY BATTS

ROUND HILL

SHEEPFOLDS

•575

RAVENSEAT
MOOR

COLDBERGH EDGE

WHITSUNDALE BECK

= coast-to-
coast route
on access land
not a public
right of way

• PILE OF STONES

COGILL
HILL

N

FB

RAVENSEAT

B6270

BIRKDALE
COMMON

ROWAN TREE GILL

NEY GILL

SHOOTING HUT

Top left; Whitsundale and two
views of Nine Standards from
the south.